Tolley s
Corporation Tax
Workbook
2006/07

by

Gina Antczak FCA CTA
Kevin Walton BA (Hons)

LexisNexis®
Tolley

Members of the LexisNexis Group worldwide

United Kingdom	LexisNexis Butterworths, a Division of Reed Elsevier (UK) Ltd, Halsbury House, 35 Chancery Lane, LONDON, WC2A 1EL, and RSH, 1–3 Baxter's Place, Leith Walk, EDINBURGH EH1 3AF
Argentina	LexisNexis Argentina, BUENOS AIRES
Australia	LexisNexis Butterworths, CHATSWOOD, New South Wales
Austria	LexisNexis Verlag ARD Orac GmbH & Co KG, VIENNA
Benelux	LexisNexis Benelux, AMSTERDAM
Canada	LexisNexis Butterworths, MARKHAM, Ontario
Chile	LexisNexis Chile Ltda, SANTIAGO
China	LexisNexis China, BEIJING AND SHANGHAI
France	LexisNexis SA, PARIS
Germany	LexisNexis Deutschland GmbH, MUNSTER
Hong Kong	LexisNexis, HONG KONG
India	LexisNexis India, NEW DELHI
Italy	Giuffrè Editore, MILAN
Japan	LexisNexis Japan, TOKYO
Malaysia	Malayan Law Journal Sdn Bhd, KUALA LUMPUR
Mexico	LexisNexis Mexico, MEXICO
New Zealand	LexisNexis NZ Ltd, WELLINGTON
Poland	Wydawnictwo Prawnicze LexisNexis Sp, WARSAW
Singapore	LexisNexis Singapore, SINGAPORE
South Africa	LexisNexis Butterworths, DURBAN
USA	LexisNexis, DAYTON, Ohio

© Reed Elsevier (UK) Ltd 2006

Published by LexisNexis Butterworths

A CIP Catalogue record for this book is available from the British Library.

ISBN 10: 0 7545 3055 8
ISBN 13: 9780 7545 3055 8

Typeset by Interactive Sciences Ltd, Gloucester
Printed in Great Britain by Hobbs the Printers Ltd, Totton, Hampshire

Visit LexisNexis Butterworths at www.lexisnexis.co.uk

About This Book

Tolley's Corporation Tax Workbook illustrates the practical application of UK corporation tax legislation through worked examples. The computations aid understanding of complex areas of the law and provide guidance on layout. Detailed explanatory notes and statutory references are provided wherever appropriate. The comprehensive index and table of statutes make it easy to find a particular computation quickly.

The Workbook is designed to be used on its own or in conjunction with Tolley's Corporation Tax, and so the chapters follow the order of the commentary in that volume.

This 2006/07 edition is fully up to date and includes the provisions of Finance Act 2006. Cross-references prefixed 'IT' and 'CGT' refer to the companion volumes Tolley's Income Tax Workbook 2006/07 and Tolley's Capital Gains Tax Workbook 2006/07.

Comments and suggestions for improvements are always welcome.

Abbreviations and References

ABBREVIATIONS

ACT	=	Advance Corporation Tax
Art	=	Article
b/f	=	brought forward
C/A	=	Court of Appeal
CAA	=	Capital Allowances Act
CCAB	=	Consultative Committee of Accountancy Bodies
C/D	=	Chancery Division
c/f	=	carried forward
CFC	=	Controlled Foreign Company
CGT	=	Capital Gains Tax
CGTA	=	Capitals Gains Tax Act 1979
CT	=	Corporation Tax
CY	=	Current Year
DTR	=	Double Tax Relief
EIS	=	Enterprise Investment Scheme
ESC	=	Extra-Statutory Concession
FA	=	Finance Act
F(No 2)A	=	Finance (No 2) Act
FIFO	=	First In, First Out
FII	=	Franked Investment Income
FY	=	Financial Year
FYA	=	First-Year Allowance
H/L	=	House of Lords
HMIT	=	Her Majesty's Inspector of Taxes
IBA	=	Industrial Buildings Allowance
ICTA	=	Income and Corporation Taxes Act 1988
IRPR	=	Inland Revenue Press Release
IT	=	Income Tax
ITTOIA	=	Income Tax (Trading and Other Income) Act
LIFO	=	Last In, First Out
NBV	=	Net Book Value
NIC	=	National Insurance Contributions
para	=	paragraph
PAYE	=	Pay As You Earn
P/e	=	Period ended
PY	=	Previous Year
Reg	=	Regulation
s	=	section
SC/S	=	Scottish Court of Session
Sch	=	Schedule
Sec	=	Section
SI	=	Statutory Instrument
SSAP	=	Statement of Standard Accounting Practice
TCGA	=	Taxation of Chargeable Gains Act 1992
TMA	=	Taxes Management Act 1970
VCT	=	Venture Capital Trust
WDA	=	Writing-down Allowance
WDV	=	Written-down Value
Y/e	=	Year ended

REFERENCES

STC	=	Simon's Tax Cases, (LexisNexis Butterworths, Halsbury House, 35 Chancery Lane, London, WC2A 1EL)
TC	=	Official Tax Cases (H.M. Stationery Office, P.O. Box 276, SW8 5DT)

Contents

101   Accounting Periods

101.1 **EFFECT OF AN ACCOUNTING PERIOD OVERLAPPING TWO FINANCIAL YEARS HAVING DIFFERENT RATES OF CORPORATION TAX** [*ICTA 1988, ss 8(3), 834(4); FA 2001, s 55; FA 2002, s 31*]

For the year ended 30 June 2002, the following information is relevant to A Ltd, a company with no associated companies.

	£
Schedule D, Case I	200,600
Schedule A	35,000
Schedule D, Case III	30,000
Charges paid (gross)	1,000 — on 31.7.01
	9,000 — on 31.3.02

The small companies' rate of corporation tax for the financial year 2001 is 20% and the rate for the financial year 2002 is 19%.

The corporation tax computation of A Ltd for the 12-month accounting period ended on 30.6.02 is

	£		
Schedule D, Case I	200,600		
Schedule A	35,000		
Schedule D, Case III	30,000		
	265,600		
Charges	10,000		
	£255,600		
Total profits apportioned			
1.7.01 – 31.3.02		$\frac{9}{12}$ × £255,600	£191,700
1.4.02 – 30.6.02		$\frac{3}{12}$ × £255,600	£63,900
Tax chargeable			
20% × £191,700			38,340
19% × £63,900			12,141
Total tax charge			£50,481

101.2 **PERIODS OF ACCOUNT EXCEEDING 12 MONTHS** [*ICTA 1988, ss 12(3), 72, 834(4)*]

B Ltd prepares accounts for 16 months ending on 31 March 2007. The following information is relevant

	£
Profit for 16 months	800,000
Schedule D, Case III income (not in respect of loan relationships) received on 1 March and 1 September each year (note (*b*))	50,000
Charitable donations paid on 1 January each year (gross)	70,000
Capital gain (after indexation) arising on 1.6.06	100,000
Tax written down value of plant and machinery main pool at 1.12.05	40,000
Plant purchased 1.2.06	200,000
Plant purchased 1.2.07	246,000
Proceeds of plant sold 31.12.06 (less than cost)	4,000

B Ltd will be chargeable to corporation tax as follows

		Accounting period 12 months to 30.11.06	Accounting period 4 months to 31.3.07
		£	£
Adjusted profits (apportioned 12:4)		600,000	200,000
Capital allowances	(note (*a*))	(90,000)	(135,167)
Schedule D, Case I		510,000	64,833
Schedule D, Case III	(note (*b*))	100,000	50,000
Chargeable gain	(note (*c*))	100,000	—
		710,000	141,833
Charges on income	(note (*d*))	(70,000)	(70,000)
Chargeable profits		£640,000	£44,833

Notes

(*a*)   Capital allowances

12 months to 30.11.06

	FYAs £	Main pool £	Allowances £
WDV b/f		40,000	
Additions	200,000		
FYA at 40%	(80,000)		80,000
	120,000		
WDA 25%		(10,000)	10,000
Transfer to main pool	(120,000)	120,000	
Total allowances			£90,000
WDV c/f		£150,000	

101.2   Accounting Periods

4 months to 31.3.06

	FYAs £	Main pool £	Allowances £
WDV b/f		150,000	
Additions	246,000		
FYA at 50%	(123,000)		123,000
	123,000		
Disposals		(4,000)	
		146,000	
WDA 25% x $\frac{4}{12}$		(12,167)	12,167
Transfer to main pool	(123,000)	123,000	
Total allowances			£135,167
WDV c/f		£256,833	

It is assumed that the conditions for the 40% and 50% first-year allowances for the additions on 1.2.06 and 1.2.07 respectively are met. Writing-down allowances, but not first-year allowances, are a proportionately reduced percentage of 25% if the accounting period is only part of a year. [*CAA 2001, s 56(3)*].

(b)   Schedule D, Case III

12 months to 30.11.06		£
	1.3.06 receipt	50,000
	1.9.06 receipt	50,000
		£100,000

4 months to 31.3.07	1.3.07 receipt	£50,000

The total amount received is not apportioned on a time basis. [*ICTA 1988, s 9(1)*]. A Schedule D, Case III charge in respect of a non-trading credit on loan relationships is in any event calculated by reference to accounting periods. [*FA 1996, s 84*].

(c)   The capital gain is not apportioned on a time basis, but is included for the period in which it arises. [*TCGA 1992, s 8(1)*].

(d)   The charges are not apportioned on a time basis, but are included for the period in which they are paid. [*ICTA 1988, s 338(1)(4); FA 2002, Sch 30 para 1(2)*].

(e)   The tax for the two accounting periods ended 30.11.06 and 31.3.07 will be due for payment on 1.9.07 and 1.1.08 respectively. [*ICTA 1988, s 10(1)(a)*]. The CT return(s) for both accounting periods will be due by 31.3.08, i.e. the first anniversary of the last day of the sixteen-month period of account, or, if later, three months after the issue of the notice requiring the return. [*FA 1998, Sch 18 para 14*]. See also 123 RETURNS.

102   Advance Corporation Tax

102.1 **SURPLUS AND SHADOW ACT** [*ICTA 1988, s 239; FA 1998, s 32; SI 1999 No 358*]

(A) How it can be used

H Ltd is a trading company with no associated companies. The company has chargeable profits for the year ending 31 December 2006 of £1,600,000. During that year it pays a dividend of £500,000. At 1 January 2006, H Ltd had surplus ACT of £300,000.

H Ltd may obtain relief in the year ended 31.12.06 for surplus ACT as follows.

	£
Maximum ACT limit (£1,600,000 @ 20%)	320,000
Less Shadow ACT (£500,000 × $\frac{20}{80}$)	125,000
ACT set-off	£195,000

Corporation tax for the y/e 31.12.06 is payable as follows.

Mainstream CT (£1,600,000 @ 30%)	480,000
Less ACT	195,000
Tax payable	£295,000

Surplus ACT memorandum

ACT brought forward at 1.1.06	300,000
Less Used y/e 31.12.06	195,000
ACT carried forward at 31.12.06	£105,000

Notes

(*a*)   The ACT set-off is restricted to the amount of ACT that would have been payable on a distribution which, together with the ACT payable in respect of it, equals the chargeable profits. For FY 1994 onwards, the rate of set-off is 20%.

(*b*)   Surplus shadow ACT is to be carried back and treated as shadow ACT in respect of distributions made in accounting periods beginning in the previous six years (but not before 6 April 1999) with unused balances carried forward. It cannot be carried back so as to displace actual surplus ACT relieved in an earlier period except for the year before the year in which the surplus shadow ACT arose.

(B) Shadow ACT and tax credits

J Ltd (which has no associated companies) pays a dividend of £1,000 on 30 June 2006 and receives a dividend of £800 on the same date.

J Ltd will have made a franked payment as follows

	£
Distribution	1,000
Shadow ACT (@ $\frac{20}{80}$)	250
Franked payment	1,250

J Ltd will have received franked investment income

Distribution	800
Tax credit (@ $\frac{100}{90}$)	89
Franked investment income	889

Amount available to set against franked payments (FII × $\frac{9}{8}$)	1,000
Shadow ACT treated as paid ((1,250 − 1,000) × 20%)	50

Note

(a)   Where franked investment income ('FII') is received in an accounting period after 5 April 1999, or surplus FII is brought forward (including surplus arising before 6 April 1999), shadow ACT is only treated as being paid in that period to the extent that franked distributions (i.e. £1,000 + £250 = £1,250) exceed the sum of nine-eighths of the FII received (£889 × 98 = £1,000) and the amount of any surplus FII brought forward.

102.2 GROUPS OF COMPANIES

For an example on the allocation of surplus shadow ACT within groups of companies, see 110.1 GROUPS OF COMPANIES.

103   Capital Allowances

103.1 **TRANSFER OF TRADE WITHIN GROUP: PERIOD OF ACCOUNT EXCEEDING 12 MONTHS** [*ICTA 1988, s 343; CAA 2001, ss 55, 56, 310–313, Sch 2 para 26*]

A Ltd owns 80% of the ordinary share capital of both B Ltd and C Ltd, the latter companies carrying on similar trades.

A Ltd and C Ltd prepare accounts annually to 31 July. B Ltd which previously prepared accounts to 30 April each year has prepared accounts for 15 months ending on 31 July 2006.

On 31 December 2005, C Ltd transferred the whole of its trade to B Ltd under circumstances covered by *ICTA 1988, s 343*.

The following information is relevant to B Ltd

		£
Trading profit for 15 months to 31.7.06		200,000
1.5.05	Tax written-down value of plant and machinery main pool	5,800
11.6.05	Plant purchased	3,000
3.9.05	Plant purchased	2,000
4.10.05	Plant sold (original cost £9,000)	6,800
1.3.06	Plant purchased	8,000
10.5.06	Plant sold (original cost £40,000)	22,568
15.6.06	Plant purchased	30,000
1.8.05	Tax written-down value of plant and machinery main pool owned by C Ltd	9,216
Original cost of four-year old building, owned by C Ltd and qualifying for industrial buildings writing-down allowances		300,000

B Ltd is not entitled to first-year allowances on the plant purchased as it is a member of a 'large group' and the plant is not energy-saving or environmentally beneficial plant or machinery (see *CAA 2001, ss 45A, 45H, 47*).

B Ltd will have chargeable profits as follows

	Accounting period 12 months to 30.4.06	Accounting period 3 months to 31.7.06
	£	£
Trading profits	160,000	40,000
Capital allowances on plant and machinery	(3,688)	(1,500)
Industrial buildings allowance	(4,000)	(3,000)
Chargeable profits	£152,312	£35,500

103.1　Capital Allowances

Capital allowances

Plant and machinery

12 months to 30.4.06

	Main pool £	Total allowances £
WDV b/f	5,800	
Additions	13,000	
Transfer from C Ltd note (a)	8,256	
	27,056	
Disposals	(6,800)	
	20,256	
WDA on assets transferred from C Ltd £8,256 × 25% × $\frac{4}{12}$ note (a)	(688)	688
WDA on balance of expenditure £(20,256 − 8,256) × 25%	(3,000)	3,000
WDV c/f	£16,568	
Total allowances		£3,688

3 months to 31.7.06

	Main Pool £	Allowances £
WDV b/f	16,568	
Additions	30,000	
	46,568	
Disposals	(22,568)	
	24,000	
WDA (25% × $\frac{3}{12}$)	1,500	£1,500
WDV c/f	£22,500	

Industrial building	Allowances
12 months to 30.4.06 £300,000 × 4% × $\frac{4}{12}$	£4,000
3 months to 31.7.06 £300,000 × 4% × $\frac{3}{12}$	£3,000

Notes

(a) Where a trade is transferred part-way through an accounting period, HMRC take the view that writing-down allowances are calculated for the predecessor for a notional accounting period ending on the date of the transfer. The successor is then treated, in relation to the assets transferred, as having a chargeable period starting on that date and running to the end of its accounting period. (HMRC Capital Allowances Manual CA 15400.)

		£
The transfer value of machinery and plant obtained from C Ltd is		
Tax written-down value at 1.8.05		9,216
WDA due to C Ltd (£9,216 × 25% × $\frac{5}{12}$)		960
		£8,256

(b)   The 'successor' company (B Ltd) is entitled to the capital allowances which the 'predecessor' company (C Ltd) would have been able to claim if it had continued to trade. [*ICTA 1988, s 343(1)(2); CAA 2001, Sch 2 para 26*].

(c)   No first-year or initial allowance is otherwise available to the successor on assets transferred to it by the predecessor. [*ICTA 1988, s 343(2)(b)(ii); CAA 2001, Sch 2 para 26*].

(d)   Writing-down allowances are reduced proportionately where the accounting period is less than one year. [*CAA 2001, ss 56(3), 310(2)*].

103.2   Capital Allowances

103.2 **NO CLAIM FOR FIRST-YEAR AND WRITING-DOWN ALLOWANCES** [*CAA 2001, ss 52(4), 56(5)*]

D Ltd is a company with one wholly-owned subsidiary, E Ltd, and no other associated companies. Both companies prepare accounts to 30 September. For the year ended 30 September 2006, D Ltd has trading profits of £100,000 before capital allowances, whilst E Ltd incurs a trading loss of £100,000. E Ltd also incurred trading losses in the previous year and is unlikely to have any taxable profits in the foreseeable future. In the year to 30 September 2006, D Ltd spent £100,000 on plant and machinery on 26 April 2006, which qualifies for first-year allowances at 50%. There was a written-down value of £70,000 on the plant and machinery main pool at 1 October 2005 and there were no disposals during the year.

Assuming a group relief claim is made under *ICTA 1988, s 402* and that D Ltd claims the full capital allowances to which it is entitled, D Ltd's Schedule D, Case I computation for the year to 30 September 2006 will be as follows

	£
Trading profit	100,000
Less capital allowances (see below)	67,500
	32,500
Less loss surrendered by E Ltd	32,500
Taxable profit	Nil

E Ltd has unrelieved losses carried forward of £67,500 which will not be relieved in the foreseeable future.

D Ltd's capital allowances computation is as follows

	Expenditure qualifying for FYAs £	Main pool £	Total allowances £
WDV b/f		70,000	
Additions	100,000		
FYA 50%	(50,000)		50,000
WDA 25%		(17,500)	17,500
	50,000	52,500	
Transfer to main pool	(50,000)	50,000	
WDV c/f		£102,500	
Total allowances			£67,500

If D Ltd does not claim capital allowances, the position is as follows

	£
Trading profit	100,000
Less loss surrendered by E Ltd	100,000
Taxable profit	Nil

Capital allowances computation

	Expenditure qualifying for FYAs £	Main pool £	Total allowances £
WDV b/f		70,000	
Additions	—	100,000	—
		170,000	
WDA – not claimed		—	—
WDV c/f		£170,000	
Total allowances			Nil

Notes

(*a*)   A company may claim whatever allowances it chooses, if any. [*CAA 2001, ss 52(4), 56(5)*]. If a person, including a company, does not claim a first-year allowance, where available, the expenditure qualifies for writing-down allowances in the same accounting period. Before *CAA 2001* had effect (i.e. for corporation tax purposes, for accounting periods ending before 1 April 2001) this applied only if the person so elected, within two years after the end of the accounting period. [*CAA 2001, s 58*]. Capital allowances claims may be withdrawn within the same time limits as apply to the making of claims. [*FA 1998, s 117, Sch 18 paras 78–83; CAA 2001, Sch 2 para 103*].

(*b*)   As a result of the allowances not being claimed, all of E Ltd's current year losses have been relieved, and D Ltd has a higher written-down value to carry forward on its plant and machinery main pool.

(*c*)   It is assumed that D Ltd and E Ltd together constitute a 'small' enterprise and meet the other conditions for the 50% first-year allowances for expenditure incurred after 31 March 2006 and before 1 April 2007 and that all of the expenditure was incurred on assets qualifying for that allowance.

(*d*)   See 110.2 – 110.6 GROUPS OF COMPANIES for group relief generally.

104   Capital Gains

104.1 **CAPITAL LOSSES** [*TCGA 1992, s 8(1)*]

P Ltd has the following capital gains/(losses)

Year ended		£
31.7.03	Gains	27,000
	Losses	(7,000)
31.7.04	Losses	(12,000)
31.7.05	Gains	5,000
	Losses	(13,000)
31.7.06	Gains	40,000
	Losses	(30,000)

The gains and losses would be dealt with as follows in the CT computations of P Ltd

	£	Gain assessable £
31.7.03		
Gains assessable to CT		£20,000
31.7.04		
Unrelieved losses carried forward	£(12,000)	Nil
31.7.05		
Losses (net)	8,000	Nil
Add Unrelieved losses brought forward	12,000	
Unrelieved losses carried forward	£(20,000)	
31.7.06		
Chargeable gains (net)	10,000	
Deduct Unrelieved losses brought forward	20,000	
Unrelieved losses carried forward	£(10,000)	Nil

Notes

(a)   Unrelieved losses cannot be set off against trading profits, but are available to relieve future gains.

(b)   Gains otherwise assessable to CT may be covered by trading losses for the same accounting period or trading losses carried back from a succeeding period under *ICTA 1988, s 393A(1)*—see 118 LOSSES.

(c)   See also 104.3(A) below.

104.2 CLOSE COMPANY TRANSFERRING ASSET AT UNDERVALUE [*TCGA 1992, s 125*]

(A)

G Ltd (a close company) sold a building in 2005 to an associated company Q Ltd, which is not a member of the same group as G Ltd, at a price below market value at the time. Relevant values relating to the asset were

	£
Cost 1992	45,000
Market value at date of disposal	95,000
Sale proceeds received	75,000

The issued share capital of G Ltd was held at the time of disposal as follows

	£1 ordinary shares	Value prior to sale of asset £
C	25,000	50,000
D	30,000	60,000
E	20,000	40,000
F	25,000	50,000
	100,000	£200,000

Sale proceeds on subsequent sale (at market value) in July 2006 of C's total shareholding (originally purchased at £0.80 per share in 1990) in G Ltd were £55,000.

G Ltd's chargeable gain on the sale of the building in 2005 is

	£
Market value note (*c*)	95,000
Cost	45,000
Unindexed gain	50,000
Indexation allowance at, say, 40% on £45,000	18,000
Chargeable gain	£32,000

C's gain on the disposal of the shares in 2006 is

	£	£
Sale proceeds		55,000
Deduct Allowable cost:		
Purchase price (25,000 × £0.80)	20,000	
Less Apportioned undervalue (note (*a*))	5,000	15,000
Unindexed gain		40,000
Indexation allowance at, say, 30% on £15,000		4,500
Chargeable gain (subject to taper relief)		£35,500

104.2 Capital Gains

Notes

(a) The apportionment of undervalue on disposal is

		£
Market value at time of sale		95,000
Deduct Sale proceeds		75,000
		£20,000

	Proportion of shareholding	Value apportioned £
C	$\frac{25}{100} \times £20,000$	5,000
D	$\frac{30}{100} \times £20,000$	6,000
E	$\frac{20}{100} \times £20,000$	4,000
F	$\frac{25}{100} \times £20,000$	5,000
		£20,000

(b) Indexation allowance is computed by reference to the allowable cost as reduced by the apportioned undervalue. [*TCGA 1992, s 53(3)*].

(c) In the computation of the company's gain, market value is substituted for proceeds under *TCGA 1992, s 17*.

(d) Transfers of assets on or before 31 March 1982 are disregarded in respect of disposals after 5 April 1988 to which re-basing applies (not illustrated in this example). [*TCGA 1992, s 125(1)(5)*].

(B)

Assume the same facts as in (A) above except that the building had a market value of £155,000 at the date of disposal and C subsequently sold his shares for their market value of £40,000. Assume now also that C purchased his shares at £0.70 per share before 31 March 1982 and that their value on that date was £21,000.

G Ltd's chargeable gain will be computed under the same principles as in (A) above.

C's gain on the disposal of the shares will be as follows

(i) By reference to cost

	£	£
Sale proceeds		40,000
Deduct Allowable cost:		
Purchase price (25,000 × £0.70)	17,500	
Less Apportioned undervalue (note (a)) 20,000		—
Unindexed gain		40,000
Indexation allowance (note (b))		1,047
Gain after indexation		£38,953

(ii) By reference to 31.3.82 value

	£	£
Sale proceeds		40,000
Deduct Allowable cost:		
31 March 1982 value	21,000	
Less Apportioned undervalue (note (*a*))	20,000	
		1,000
Unindexed gain		39,000
Indexation at 104.7% on £1,000 (note (*b*))		1,047
Gain after indexation		£37,953

Chargeable gain (subject to taper relief)	£37,953

Notes

(*a*) The apportionment of undervalue on disposal is

	£
Market value at time of sale	155,000
Deduct Sale proceeds	75,000
	£80,000

	Proportion of shareholding	Value apportioned £
C	$\frac{25}{100} \times £80,000$	20,000
D	$\frac{30}{100} \times £80,000$	24,000
E	$\frac{20}{100} \times £80,000$	16,000
F	$\frac{25}{100} \times £80,000$	20,000
		£80,000

(*b*) Unless an election under *TCGA 1992, s 35(5)* for universal rebasing at 31.3.82 is in force, indexation is by reference to the higher of cost and 31.3.82 value (as reduced by the apportioned undervalue in either case). [*TCGA 1992, s 55(2)*].

Indexation allowance is given up to April 1998 after which taper relief applies.

(*c*) See also notes (*b*) and (*d*) to (A) above.

104.3   Capital Gains

(A) Notional intra-group transfers of assets [*TCGA 1992, s 171A; FA 2000, s 101; FA 2001, s 77*]

A Ltd and B Ltd are members of the same group of companies, preparing accounts each year to 31 March. On 30 September 2006, A Ltd sold an asset (asset 1) to an unconnected third party for £100,000. The asset had been acquired in June 2002 for £40,000. On 29 January 2007 B Ltd sold an asset (asset 2), which had cost £70,000 in January 2000, for £50,000 to C Ltd, an unconnected third party. B Ltd incurred costs on the disposal of £2,000. Neither company disposes of any other assets in the year ended 31 March 2007.

A Ltd and B Ltd jointly elect before 31 March 2009 under *TCGA 1992, s 171A* for asset 2 to be treated as transferred to A Ltd immediately before its disposal to C Ltd.

The chargeable gains computations for the year ended 31 March 2007 for A Ltd and B Ltd are as follows.

B Ltd

Deemed disposal of asset 2 in January 2007: consideration deemed to be such that neither gain nor loss arises.

	£
Deemed consideration	84,000
Cost of asset to B Ltd	70,000
Indexation allowance £70,000 × say 20%	14,000
Gain	—

A Ltd
Disposal of asset 1

	£
Consideration	100,000
Cost	40,000
Indexation allowance £40,000 × say 10%	4,000
Chargeable gain	£56,000

Deemed disposal of asset 2

	£	£
Consideration		50,000
Cost to A Ltd	84,000	
Less indexation allowance previously given	14,000	(70,000)
Cost of disposal incurred by B Ltd		(2,000)
Allowable loss		£(22,000)

Net chargeable gains £56,000 − £22,000 = £34,000

Note
(*a*)   The election under *TCGA 1992, s 171A* must be made in writing to an officer of the Board within two years after the end of the accounting period of B Ltd in which the actual disposal of asset 2 was made, and can only be made if an actual transfer of

the asset (or part) from B Ltd to A Ltd would have been a no gain, no loss disposal within *TCGA 1992, s 171*.

(B) Intra-group transfers of assets which are trading stock of one company but not of the other — transfer from a 'capital asset' company to a 'trading stock' company
[*TCGA 1992, ss 161, 173(1); FA 2000, s 102, Sch 29 para 11*]
In June 2006, X Ltd transfers an item classed as a fixed asset to another group company Y Ltd, which treats it as trading stock.

The following information is relevant

	Case (i)	Case (ii)
	£	£
Original cost (after 31.3.82)	100,000	100,000
Market value at date of transfer	120,000	40,000
Eventual sale proceeds	140,000	140,000
Indexation allowance due on original cost at date of transfer	17,000	17,000

The position of Y Ltd will be as follows if there is no election under *TCGA 1992, s 161(3)*

Chargeable gain/(allowable loss) on appropriation

Market value	120,000	40,000
Deemed cost of asset (note (*a*))	117,000	117,000
Gain/(loss)	3,000	(77,000)
Deduct Indexation allowance included in cost (note (*b*))	—	17,000
Chargeable gain/(allowable loss)	£3,000	£(60,000)
Trading profit at date of sale		
Sale proceeds	140,000	140,000
Deemed cost of asset	120,000	40,000
Trading profit	£20,000	£100,000

With an election under *TCGA 1992, s 161(3)*

No chargeable gain or allowable loss arises on appropriation

	£	£	£	£
Trading profit at date of sale				
Sale proceeds		140,000		140,000
Market value at appropriation	120,000		40,000	
Adjustment for (gain)/loss otherwise (chargeable)/allowable	(3,000)	117,000	60,000	100,000
Trading profit		£23,000		£40,000

Notes
(*a*) The intra-group transfer by X Ltd to Y Ltd is treated as a disposal on which neither a gain nor a loss accrues after taking account of any indexation allowance due. X Ltd has no liability on the transfer and Y Ltd has a deemed acquisition cost of £117,000 on the appropriation to stock. [*TCGA 1992, ss 56(2), 171(1); FA 1994, s 93(5)(a)*].

104.3   Capital Gains

(b)   The indexation allowance on a no gain/no loss transfer must be excluded on a subsequent disposal to the extent that it would otherwise contribute to an allowable loss. [*TCGA 1992, s 56(3); FA 1994, s 93(5)(b)*].

(c)   In Case (ii), with an election under *section 161(3)*, the adjustment for the loss cannot include any 'pre-entry loss'. [*TCGA 1992, Sch 7A para 10; FA 1993, s 88, Sch 8*]. It is assumed there is no pre-entry loss in this example. See (F) below for pre-entry losses generally.

(C) Intra-group transfers of assets which are trading stock of one company but not of the other — transfer from a 'trading stock' company to a 'capital asset' company [*TCGA 1992, ss 161, 173(2)*]

P Ltd acquires from another group company Q Ltd as a fixed asset an item previously treated as trading stock.

	£
Cost to Q Ltd (after 31.3.82)	100,000
Market value at date of transfer	150,000
Eventual sale proceeds	200,000
Indexation allowance due on transfer	
value from date of transfer to date of sale	10,000

The group will have the following trading profits and chargeable gains

	£	£
Q Ltd trading profit [*TCGA 1992, s 161(2)*]		
Deemed sale proceeds		150,000
Cost to Q Ltd		100,000
Trading profit		£50,000
P Ltd chargeable gain [*TCGA 1992, s 171(1)*]		
Sale proceeds		200,000
Cost of asset	150,000	
Indexation allowance	10,000	
		160,000
Chargeable gain		£40,000

(D) Rollover relief on the replacement of business assets [*TCGA 1992, ss 152, 153, 155, 175; FA 1995, s 48; FA 2000, Sch 29 para 10*]
M Ltd and N Ltd are 75% subsidiaries of H Ltd. On 1 February 2005 M Ltd sold a showroom for £200,000, realising a chargeable gain of £110,000. N Ltd purchased a factory for £150,000 in March 2007, within three years after the date of sale of the showroom.

Rollover relief could be claimed as follows

	£	£
Gain otherwise chargeable to corporation tax		110,000
Deduct Unrelieved gain:		
Sale proceeds	200,000	
Less Amount reinvested	150,000	
Chargeable gain	£50,000	50,000
Rollover relief		£60,000

New base cost of factory

Purchase price	150,000
Deduct Rollover relief	60,000
	£90,000

Notes

(*a*)   To qualify for relief, the two companies concerned need not be members of the same group throughout the period between the transactions but each must be a member at the time of its own particular transaction.

(*b*)   N Ltd will be entitled to an indexation allowance, based on the deemed cost of £90,000, on a subsequent sale (to the extent that such sale produces an unindexed gain).

(*c*)   See also CGT 204.2 ASSETS HELD ON 31 MARCH 1982 and CGT 222 ROLLOVER RELIEF.

(E) A company ceasing to be a member of a group [*TCGA 1992, ss 171(1), 179(1)(3)(4), 179A, 179B, Sch 7AB; FA 1993, s 89; FA 1995, s 49; FA 2001, Sch 29 para 4; FA 2002, ss 42, 43, Sch 7*]
A Ltd had the following transactions

1.3.80   Purchased a freehold property £10,000.
31.3.82   Market value £25,000.
1.12.00   Sold the freehold to B Ltd (a wholly-owned subsidiary) for £20,000 (market value £80,000).
31.7.06   Sold its interest in B Ltd (at which time B Ltd continued to own the freehold property).

Both companies prepare accounts to 30 April.

104.3 Capital Gains

Relevant values of the RPI are: March 1982: 79.44, December 2000: 172.2.

The taxation consequences are
(i) There will be no chargeable gain on A Ltd's disposal of the property to B Ltd as the disposal is one on which, after taking account of the indexation allowance, neither gain nor loss arises. [*TCGA 1992, ss 56(2), 171(1); FA 1994, s 93(5)(a)*].

Indexation factor

$$\frac{172.2 - 79.44}{79.44} = 1.168$$

	£
Cost to A Ltd	10,000
Indexation allowance £25,000 × 1.168 (note (*a*))	29,200
Deemed cost to B Ltd	£39,200

(ii) Following the sale of A Ltd's shares in B Ltd on 31.7.06 (i.e. within six years after the transaction in (i) above), B Ltd will have a deemed disposal as follows.

Deemed disposal on 1.12.00

	£	£	£
Market value at 1.12.00		80,000	80,000
Cost (as above)	39,200		
Less indexation to date	29,200		
		10,000	
Market value at 31.3.82			25,000
Unindexed gain		70,000	55,000
Indexation allowance			
£25,000 × 1.168		29,200	29,200
Indexed gain		£40,800	£25,800
Chargeable gain subject to CT			£25,800
B Ltd's new base cost for future gains			£80,000

Although the deemed disposal occurs on 1 December 2000, i.e. immediately after B Ltd's acquisition, the gain is treated as accruing on 1 May 2006, i.e. the beginning of the accounting period in which B Ltd left the group, being later than the date of the deemed disposal. The gain thus forms part of B Ltd's profits for the year ended 30 April 2007.

Notes
(*a*) The indexation allowance on the no gain/no loss transfer is calculated by reference to the market value at 31 March 1982 as this is higher than the original cost. [*TCGA 1992, s 55(1)(2)*].

(*b*) For re-basing purposes, B Ltd is deemed to have held the asset at 31 March 1982. [*TCGA 1992, Sch 3 para 1*]. *TCGA 1992, s 55(5)(6)* apply in the computation of B Ltd's chargeable gain.

(*c*) Where a company ceases to be a member of a group on or after 1 April 2002, an election can be made for all or part of a gain or loss arising under *TCGA 1992, s 179* to be treated as arising to another company which was a member of the group at the time the gain or loss is treated as accruing. The election required is a joint election by both the company leaving the group and the company to whom the gain or loss is to be deemed to accrue. The latter company must be resident in the UK or own assets within the charge to corporation tax on chargeable gains. [*TCGA 1992, s 179A; FA 2002, s 42*].

(*d*)   Where a company ceases to be a member of a group on or after 1 April 2002 and the gain arising under *TCGA 1992, s 179* results from the deemed disposal of an asset that is a qualifying asset within *TCGA 1992, s 155* (rollover relief on the replacement of business assets), the company may claim rollover relief in respect of the gain (subject to the acquisition of a qualifying replacement asset). The rollover relief provisions are modified for this purpose. [*TCGA 1992, s 179B, Sch 7AB; FA 2002, s 43, Sch 7*]. See CGT 222 for rollover relief generally.

(F) Restriction on set-off of pre-entry losses [*TCGA 1992, s 177A, Sch 7A; FA 1993, s 88, Sch 8; FA 1994, ss 93(8)–(11), 94; FA 2006, s 70(3)*]
C Ltd has a 100% subsidiary, D Ltd. D Ltd acquired a 100% subsidiary, E Ltd, on 1 April 2002 and a 75% subsidiary, F Ltd, on 1 April 2004. All the companies prepare their accounts to 31 March. The following information is relevant (neither E Ltd nor F Ltd having realised any gains or losses except as stated).

(i)   At 1 April 2002, E Ltd had unrelieved capital losses of £120,000 and its assets included a freehold property which it had acquired on 1 July 1998 for £700,000 and on which it had incurred enhancement expenditure of £100,000 on 1 October 1999. The property was valued at £700,000 at 1 April 2002. During the year ended 31 March 2006, E Ltd realised chargeable gains of £30,000 on assets held at 1 April 2002 and it also realised an allowable loss of £10,000 on an asset purchased on 31 May 2002. On 1 October 2006, the company sold the above-mentioned freehold property for £550,000.

(ii)   F Ltd had no capital losses brought forward at 1 April 2004. At that date, it held 100,000 ordinary shares in XYZ plc, a quoted company. It had acquired 60,000 of these on 1 May 1998 for £100,000 and 40,000 on 1 June 2002 for £70,000. The shares had an indexed pool value of £188,230 at 1 April 2004, and their market value at that date was £110,000. On 1 November 2004, F Ltd acquired a further 50,000 XYZ ordinary shares for £30,000 and on 31 August 2006 it sold 120,000 such shares for £60,000.

F Ltd also made two disposals other than of XYZ shares during the year to 31 March 2007, realising chargeable gains on each. The first disposal, on which the gain was £55,000, was of an asset acquired by transfer from C Ltd (at no gain/no loss by virtue of *TCGA 1992, s 171*). The second, on which the gain was £35,000 was acquired from outside the group in December 2004 and used since that time in F Ltd's trade, which has continued unchanged since 31 March 2004.

The provisions restricting set-off of pre-entry losses have the following effects

(i) E Ltd

For the year to 31.3.06, E Ltd may elect (before 1 April 2008) for the whole of the £30,000 gain to be regarded as covered by pre-entry losses. The £100,000 losses carried forward at 31.3.06 then comprise pre-entry losses of £90,000 and other losses of £10,000. In the absence of an election, losses are set against gains on a first in/first out basis for these purposes, so the same result would accrue in this case. [*TCGA 1992, Sch 7A para 6(2)–(4)*].

The £90,000 pre-entry losses are carried forward and may be set only against gains on other assets held by E Ltd immediately before 1.4.02 or gains on assets acquired by it on or after that date from outside the group and not used or held for any purposes other than

21

those of the trade carried on by E Ltd immediately before that date and which continued to be carried on by it up to the date of disposal. [*TCGA 1992, Sch 7A para 7(1)*].

The overall loss on the disposal of the freehold property is as follows

	£	£
Proceeds (1.10.06)		550,000
Cost (1.7.98)	700,000	
Enhancement expenditure (1.10.99)	100,000	800,000
Allowable loss		£250,000

The pre-entry proportion of the allowable loss is calculated as follows

$$£250,000 \times \frac{700,000}{800,000} \times \frac{3y\ 9m\ (1.7.98-1.4.02)}{8y\ 3m\ (1.7.98-1.10.06)} \quad = \quad 99,432$$

$$£250,000 \times \frac{100,000}{800,000} \times \frac{2y\ 6m\ (1.10.99-1.4.02)}{7y\ 0m\ (1.10.99-1.10.06)} \quad = \quad 11,161$$

	£
Pre-entry proportion	£110,593
Balance of allowable loss	£139,407

[*TCGA 1992, Sch 7A para 2; FA 1994, s 93(8)*].

E Ltd may elect (before 1 April 2009) to use an alternative method of computing the pre-entry proportion of the allowable loss, as follows

	£	£
Market value (1.4.02)		700,000
Cost (1.7.98)	700,000	
Enhancement expenditure (1.10.99)	100,000	800,000
Pre-entry proportion of allowable loss		£100,000
Balance of allowable loss (£250,000 − £100,000)		£150,000

[*TCGA 1992, Sch 7A para 5; FA 1994, s 93(10)*].

The whole of the loss of £250,000 is available for carry-forward but the pre-entry proportion of the allowable loss (£100,000 on the assumption that the election under *Sch 7A para 5* is made) can be set only against the same types of gain against which the pre-entry losses of £90,000 can be set (see above).

(ii) F Ltd

Allowable loss on XYZ plc ordinary shares

	Number of shares	Qualifying expenditure £	Indexed pool £
Acquisition 1.5.98	60,000	100,000	
Acquisition 1.6.02	40,000	70,000	
At 1.4.04	100,000	170,000	187,380
Indexed rise to 1.11.04:			
£187,380 × 0.018			3,373
Acquisition 1.11.04	50,000	30,000	30,000
	150,000	200,000	220,753
Indexed rise to 31.8.06:			
£220,753 × say 0.070			15,453
			236,206
Disposal 31.8.06	(120,000)	(160,000)	(188,965)
Pool carried forward	3,000	£40,000	£47,241

	£
Proceeds 31.8.06	60,000
Cost	160,000
Allowable loss	£100,000

Indexation allowance would be £28,965 (£188,965 − £160,000), but indexation allowance cannot increase an allowable loss. [*TCGA 1992, s 53(2A); FA 1994, s 93(3)(11)*].

Pre-entry proportion of allowable loss

Stage 1 [*TCGA 1992, Sch 7A para 3*]

The proportion of the pool disposed of (120,000 shares) exceeds the proportion *not* referable to pre-entry assets (50,000 shares). The excess of 70,000 shares is regarded as a separate asset made up as follows

	Cost £
60,000 shares acquired 1.5.98	100,000
10,000 shares acquired 1.6.02 (£70,000 × $\frac{1}{4}$)	17,500
	£117,500

	£
Proceeds of 70,000 shares £60,000 × $\frac{7}{12}$	35,000
Cost as above	117,500
Notional allowable loss on pre-entry assets	£82,500

23

104.3　Capital Gains

The pre-entry proportion of the allowable loss under *TCGA 1992, Sch 7A para 3* is calculated as follows

		£
$£82,500 \times \dfrac{100,000}{117,500} \times \dfrac{5y\ 11m\ (1.5.98\text{–}1.4.04)}{8y\ 4m\ (1.5.98\text{–}31.8.06)}$	=	49,851
$£82,500 \times \dfrac{17,500}{117,500} \times \dfrac{1y\ 10m\ (1.6.02\text{–}1.4.04)}{4y\ 3m\ (1.6.02\text{–}31.8.06)}$	=	5,300
Pre-entry proportion of allowable loss (subject to below)		£55,151

Stage 2 [TCGA 1992, Sch 7A para 4; FA 1994, s 93(9)]

		£
The amount deductible in computing the allowable loss is	(I)	160,000
The amount deductible which is attributable to the post-entry element of the disposal (50,000 shares acquired on 1.11.04) is	(II)	30,000

As (I) exceeds (II), an adjustment is required to the figure calculated at *Stage 1* above, as follows

	£	£
Expenditure actually allowed		160,000
Deduct Actual cost of assets disposed of:		
pre-entry element (see *Stage 1* above)	117,500	
post-entry element (see (II) above)	30,000	147,500
Excess		£12,500

The excess is added to the pre-entry proportion as calculated at *Stage 1* above. The pre-entry proportion of the allowable loss is thus

	£
£55,151 + £12,500 =	£67,651

(Because an adjustment is required under *TCGA 1992, Sch 7A para 4*, the election for the alternative method under *TCGA 1992, Sch 7A para 5* is *not* available. [*TCGA 1992, Sch 7A para 4(5)*]. If the election *had been* available, the calculation would have been as follows

	£
Market value of 100,000 shares held at 1.4.04	110,000
Unindexed pool value at 1.4.04	170,000
Notional loss on 100,000 shares	£60,000

As only 70,000 of the 100,000 shares held at 1.4.04 are regarded as included in the disposal on 31.8.06 (see *Stage 1* above), the pre-entry proportion of the allowable loss would have been £60,000 × $\frac{7}{10}$ = £42,000. [*TCGA 1992, Sch 7A para 5(4)–(6)*].)

Stage 3 [TCGA 1992, Sch 7A para 4(6)–(8)]

As the adjustment at *Stage 2* applies, F Ltd may elect (before 1 April 2009) that the pre-entry proportion of the loss calculated at *Stage 2* (£67,651) be reduced to the amount of the 'alternative pre-entry loss', if lower. In calculating the alternative pre-entry loss, *Stage 1* is recomputed as if the disposal was primarily of pre-entry assets, as follows

	Cost £
60,000 shares acquired 1.5.98	100,000
40,000 shares acquired 1.6.02	70,000
	£170,000

	£
Proceeds of 100,000 shares £60,000 × $\frac{10}{12}$	50,000
Cost as above	170,000
Notional allowable loss on pre-entry assets	£120,000

The pre-entry proportion of the allowable loss is calculated as follows

		£
$£120,000 \times \dfrac{100,000}{170,000} \times \dfrac{5\text{y } 11\text{m } (1.5.98-1.4.04)}{8\text{y } 4\text{m } (1.5.98-31.8.06)}$	=	50,118
$£120,000 \times \dfrac{70,000}{170,000} \times \dfrac{1\text{y } 10\text{m } (1.6.02-1.4.04)}{4\text{y } 3\text{m } (1.6.02-31.8.06)}$	=	21,315
Alternative pre-entry loss (subject to below)		£71,433

In fact, the alternative loss is higher than the pre-entry proportion of the allowable loss calculated at *Stage 2* (£67,651), so, subject to *Stage 4*, the election would not be made.

Stage 4 [TCGA 1992, Sch 7A paras 4(6)–(8), 5(4)–(6)]

In making an election under *Stage 3*, F Ltd may specify that the alternative method under *TCGA 1992, Sch 7A para 5* (as amended by *FA 1994, s 93(10)*) be used, as follows

	£
Market value of 100,000 shares held at 1.4.04	110,000
Unindexed pool value at 1.4.04	170,000
Notional loss on 100,000 shares	£60,000

As all the 100,000 shares held at 1.4.04 are regarded as included in the disposal on 31.8.06 (see *Stage 3*), the alternative pre-entry loss is £60,000. It is therefore beneficial for F Ltd to make the election mentioned at *Stage 3*, imputing an election under *TCGA 1992, Sch 7A para 5*.

104.3 Capital Gains

The pre-entry proportion of the allowable loss is then
reduced from £67,651 (*Stage 2*) to £60,000

Balance of allowable loss is £100,000 − £60,000 = £40,000

Utilisation of losses [TCGA 1992, Sch 7A paras 6(1), 7(1)(2)]

The pre-entry loss may be set against the gain of £35,000. It may not be set against the gain of £55,000. The balance of the allowable loss can be set against the gain of £55,000. F Ltd's chargeable gains for the year ended 31.3.07 are therefore as follows

	£	£
Total gains		90,000
Deduct Pre-entry losses	35,000	
Other allowable losses	40,000	75,000
Chargeable gains		£15,000
Losses carried forward (all pre-entry losses) £(60,000 − 35,000)		£25,000

Notes

(a) Broadly, the provisions of *TCGA 1992, Sch 7A* restrict the use of losses realised by a company before it joins a group and remaining unrelieved at that time and of losses on assets held at the time the company joined the group and subsequently realised. Such pre-entry losses can be set only against gains on assets held by the company at the time it joined the group or subsequently acquired by the company from outside the group and used by it in a continuing trade.

(b) The provisions apply in respect of the offset of losses against gains arising on disposals after 15 March 1993. They do not apply where the company joined the group before 1 April 1987. [*FA 1993, s 88(3)*]. The provisions do not apply where *TCGA 1992, s 184A* (restrictions on buying losses: avoidance schemes) applies. [*TCGA 1992, Sch 7A para 1(1); FA 2006, s 70(3)*].

(G) Restriction on set-off of losses against pre-entry gains [*TCGA 1992, s 177B, Schs 7A, 7AA; FA 1998, s 137, Sch 24; FA 2006, s 70*]
G Ltd has a 100% subsidiary, H Ltd. On 1 May 2005, G Ltd acquires from A Ltd, all the shares in its two wholly-owned subsidiaries, B Ltd and C Ltd. Before that date, on 1 March 2005, C Ltd had sold an asset realising a gain of £120,000. All companies make up accounts to the year ending 31 December.

On 1 June 2005, B Ltd transfers machinery to C Ltd for its net book value of £150,000 and on the same date, H Ltd transfers a freehold property and a leasehold property to C Ltd. All these assets were transferred intra-group under *TCGA 1992, s 171* and gave rise to no gain/no loss.

On 10 June 2005 C Ltd sold the freehold property realising an allowable loss of £95,000. On 12 July 2005 it sold the leasehold property realising a chargeable gain of £75,000. On 1 September 2005 C Ltd sold the machinery realising an allowable loss of £65,000.

The provisions restricting set-off of the losses against pre-entry gains have the following effects for C Ltd

Only qualifying losses may be set against the pre-entry gains of £120,000. The loss on the disposal of the machinery of £65,000 is a qualifying loss because at the entry date it was owned by a member of what had been C Ltd's group up to that time (i.e. the group of which A Ltd was the principal company). The loss of £95,000 is not a qualifying loss as it does not satisfy any of the conditions for a qualifying loss, i.e.

(a)   it is not a pre-entry loss brought forward by C Ltd;

(b)   it is not a pre-entry loss accruing to C Ltd in the gain period prior to the entry date of 1 May 2005 (either before, at the same time or after the gain accrued); and

(c)   it is not a loss occurring after 1 May 2005 but on an asset held by C Ltd or B Ltd at the entry date.

The chargeable gains of C Ltd for the year ended 31 December 2005 are computed as follows

	£	Chargeable gains £
Pre-entry gain	120,000	
Qualifying loss	(65,000)	55,000
Post-entry gains	75,000	
	(95,000)	Nil
Allowable loss carried forward	£(20,000)	
Net chargeable gains		£55,000

Without the pre-entry gains provisions, the net gain assessable would have been £35,000 (£120,000 + £75,000 − £65,000 − £95,000) with no losses to carry forward.

Notes

(a)   In calculating the chargeable gains for the period the pre-entry gain is to be adjusted for any qualifying losses. The resulting figure is then added to the chargeable gain for the whole period, calculated in the normal way (taking account of any restrictions in respect of pre-entry losses as per (E) above) but excluding all pre-entry gains and any losses which have been taken into account in arriving at the amount of the adjusted pre-entry gains, such losses not being available to carry forward.

(b)   In the adjustment of the pre-entry gain, no reduction is to be made for pre-entry losses which cannot be deducted under *TGCA 1992, Sch 7A para 7* (see (E) above) or for a loss on disposal to a connected person unless the gain arises on a disposal to the same person.

(c)   The pre-entry gains provisions apply to accounting periods ending after 17 March 1998 where the company with the pre-entry gains joined the group after that date. The provisions are repealed, broadly with effect for accounting periods ending after 4 December 2005, on the introduction of the gain buying provisions of *TCGA 1992, s 184B*. [FA 2006, s 70(4)].

(d)   Special rules apply to pooled assets (where a company has a holding of securities of the same kind which are treated as a single asset) [*TCGA 1992, s 104*] and insurance companies.

104.4   Capital Gains

104.4 **SUBSTANTIAL SHAREHOLDING EXEMPTION** [*TCGA 1992, Sch 7AC; FA 2002, s 44, Sch 8*]

Swallow Ltd acquired 1,500 shares in Summer Ltd in April 1992. Swallow Ltd holds no other investments in any company, has been a trading company throughout its existence, and is not a member of a group. Summer Ltd has 10,000 issued shares and has been a trading company since its formation. Swallow Ltd makes the following disposals of Summer Ltd shares.

31 May 2005	600 shares
30 April 2006	400 shares
30 June 2006	500 shares

The effect of the disposals for the purposes of corporation tax on chargeable gains is as follows

31 May 2005 disposal

Swallow Ltd has held at least 10% of the ordinary share capital of Summer Ltd throughout the two years prior to the disposal. The disposal is therefore of part of a substantial shareholding and no chargeable gain or allowable loss arises on the disposal.

30 April 2006 disposal

Although Swallow Ltd did not hold at least 10% of the shares in Summer Ltd immediately before the disposal (the remaining holding being only 900 of 10,000 shares), there is a twelve month period beginning within two years prior to the disposal throughout which it did hold at least 10%. That period is 1 June 2004 to 31 May 2005. Accordingly, the substantial shareholding exemption applies and no chargeable gain or allowable loss arises on the disposal.

30 June 2006 disposal

Swallow Ltd holds only 5% of the share capital of Summer Ltd immediately before the disposal. In the period from 1 July 2004 to 30 June 2006, the company held at least 10% of Summer Ltd's shares only from 1 July 2004 to 31 May 2005. This is not a continuous twelve month period beginning within two years prior to the disposal, and therefore the substantial shareholding exemption will not apply. A gain on the disposal of 500 shares will be a chargeable gain, and a loss an allowable loss.

Note

(*a*)   A gain on a disposal after 31 March 2003 by a trading company of shares in another trading company are not chargeable gains (and a loss is not an allowable loss) if, broadly, the company held at least 10% of the other company's ordinary share capital throughout a twelve month period beginning within two years prior to the disposal.

105   Close Companies

105.1 CLOSE COMPANY — DEFINITION [ICTA 1988, ss 414 – 417]

(A)

A plc is a quoted company whose ordinary share capital is owned as follows

		%
B	a director	10
C	wife of B	5
D	father of B	4
E		17
F	business partner of E	2
G	a director	10
H		8
I Ltd	a non-close company	30
J		7
100	other shareholders	7
		100

It can be shown that A plc is a close company by considering the following three steps

(i) Is A plc controlled by five or fewer participators or by its directors?

		%	%
I Ltd			30
B	own shares	10	
	C's shares	5	
	D's shares	4	
		—	19
E	own shares	17	
	F's shares	2	
		—	19
			68

As A plc is controlled by three participators, the initial conclusion is that the company is close. [ICTA 1988, ss 414(1), 416(2)].

(ii) Is A plc a quoted company, with at least 35% of the voting power owned by the public?

		%
I Ltd		30
J		7
100	other shareholders	7
		44

As at least 35% of the voting power is owned by the public it appears that A plc is exempt from close company status, subject to step (iii). [ICTA 1988, s 415(1)].

105.1   Close Companies

(iii) Is more than 85% of the voting power in A plc owned by its principal members?

	%
I Ltd	30
B	19
E	19
G	10
H	8
	86

Because the principal members own more than 85% of the voting power A plc is a close company. [*ICTA 1988, s 415(2)(6)(7)*].

Note

(*a*)   Although J owns more than 5% of the share capital, he is not a principal member because five other persons each hold more than J's 7% and so themselves constitute the principal members. [*ICTA 1988, s 415(6)*].

(B)

The ordinary share capital of A Ltd (an unquoted company) is owned as follows

		%
B	a director	9
C	son of B	9
D	works manager	5
E	wife of D	15
F	a director	9
G	a director	1
H	a director	1
J	a director	1
K	a director	1
49	other shareholders with 1% each	49
		100

A Ltd is a close company because it is controlled by its directors, thus

		%	%
B	own shares	9	
	C's shares	9	
			18
D	own shares	5	
	E's shares	15	
			20
F			9
G			1
H			1
J			1
K			1
			51

Note

(*a*)   A manager is deemed to be a director if he and his associates own 20% or more of the ordinary share capital. [*ICTA 1988, s 417(5)*].

(C)
The ordinary share capital of A Ltd is owned as follows

		%
B	a director	9
C	a director	9
D	a director	9
E		9
F		9
G Ltd	a close company	8
47	other shareholders with 1% each	47
		100

The ordinary share capital of G Ltd is owned as follows

		%
B	a director	50
C	a director	50
		100

A Ltd is not a close company under the control test because it is not under the control of five or fewer participators. The five largest shareholdings comprise only 45% of the share capital. [*ICTA 1988, ss 414(1), 416(2)*].

A Ltd is a close company under the distribution of assets test because B and C would each become entitled to one-half of G Ltd's share of the assets of A Ltd. [*ICTA 1988, s 414(2)–(2D); FA 1989, s 104*]. The shares of assets attributable to the five largest shareholdings become

		%	%
B	own share	9	
	50% of G Ltd's share	4	
			13
C	own share	9	
	50% of G Ltd's share	4	
			13
D			9
E			9
F			9
			53

31

105.1   Close Companies

(D)

A Ltd is an unquoted company with the following capital structure, owned as shown

	£1 ordinary shares	£1 non-participating preference shares (no votes attached)
B	6,000	—
C	15,000	25,000
D	6,000	19,000
E	5,000	10,000
F	1,600	13,000
G	2,000	—
Other shareholders owning less than 1,000 shares each	64,400	33,000
	100,000	100,000

The company is close by reference to share capital as follows

	Control by votes	Control of issued capital
B	6,000	6,000
C	15,000	40,000
D	6,000	25,000
E	5,000	15,000
F	—	14,600
G	2,000	—
	34,000	100,600

Note

(a)   Control of the company includes control of more than one-half of
   (i)   voting power; or
   (ii)   issued share capital.
   [*ICTA 1988, s 416(2)*].

105.2 **LOANS TO PARTICIPATORS** [*ICTA 1988, ss 419(1)(3)(4), 421(1), 826; FA 1993, s 77(4); FA 1996, s 173*]

(A)

P is a participator in Q Ltd, a close company which makes up accounts to 30 September. Q Ltd loaned P £80,000 on 29 August 2004. On 24 May 2005 P repays the loan.

The effect of these transactions on Q Ltd is as follows

1 July 2005	The company is liable to pay corporation tax of £80,000 × 25%	£20,000
31 March 2006	Q Ltd is entitled to make a claim for repayment of the corporation tax paid.	
30 June 2006	Following the claim, the company is entitled to a repayment of	£20,000

Notes

(*a*)   For loans and advances made after 5 April 1999 (following the abolition of ACT), an amount equal to 25% of the loan must be self-assessed by the company as if it were corporation tax chargeable for the accounting period in which the loan was made.

(*b*)   For loans and advances made in an accounting period ending on or after 31 March 1996 the tax is due on the day following the expiry of nine months after the end of the accounting period in which the loan or advance was made.

(*c*)   Where loans or advances, made in an accounting period ended on or after 31 March 1996, are repaid after the due date on which tax is charged, relief by claim in respect of the repayment shall not be given at any time before the expiry of nine months from the end of the accounting period in which the repayment takes place.

105.2 Close Companies

(B)

T is a participator in (but not an employee of) V Ltd, a close company. V Ltd loaned T £100,000 on 10 May 2005. On 2 March 2006, T repays £73,000 and on 15 February 2007, V Ltd agrees to waive the balance of the loan. V Ltd has a year end of 31 March and is not a large company for instalment payment purposes.

The effect of these transactions is as follows

V Ltd

On 1.1.07	The company becomes liable to pay corporation tax of (£100,000 − £73,000) £27,000 × 25%	£6,750
On 31.12.07	The company is due a repayment of £27,000 × 25%	£6,750

T

On 15.2.07	T's 2006/07 taxable income is increased by £27,000 × $\frac{10}{9}$	£30,000
	and	
	he is credited with dividend ordinary rate tax paid of £30,000 at 10%	£3,000
	If T pays tax at the higher rate, the deemed income will be subject to tax at the dividend upper rate of 32.5% on £30,000	9,750
	Less: tax credit (as above)	3,000
	T's tax liability	£6,750

Notes

(a) Where a loan or advance which gave rise to a charge under *ICTA 1988, s 419* is released or written off after 5 April 1999, a claim can be made for repayment of the tax. [*ICTA 1988, s 419(4)(4A)*].

(b) Companies are required to include *section 419* tax in their self-assessment.

34

105.3 **BENEFITS IN KIND FOR PARTICIPATORS** [*ICTA 1988, s 418*]

R is a participator in S Ltd, a close company, but he is neither a director nor an employee earning £8,500 a year or more. For the whole of 2006/07, S Ltd provided R with a new petrol fuelled car of which the 'price' for tax purposes (i.e. under *ITEPA 2003, ss 122–124*) was £21,200, and the carbon dioxide emission figure for which was 230g/km. R was required to, and did, pay S Ltd £500 a year for the use of the car. The cost of providing the car, charged in S Ltd's accounts for its year ended 31 March 2007, was £5,000.

Deemed distribution

If the benefit of the car were assessable to tax as income from employment, the cash equivalent would be

	£
£21,200 @ 33%	6,996
Less contribution	500
	£6,496

S Ltd is treated as making a distribution of £6,496 to R.

Tax credit £6,496 $\times \frac{1}{9}$ (note (*a*))	£722
Income of R for 2006/2007 £6,496 $\times \frac{10}{9}$	£7,218

Note

(*a*) The credit is non-repayable but satisfies the liability to the dividend ordinary rate (10%) on the grossed up amount and is set against a liability arising at the dividend upper rate (32.5%).

S Ltd's taxable profits

In computing S Ltd's profits chargeable to corporation tax, the actual expenditure charged (£5,000) must be added back.

106   Controlled Foreign Companies

106.1   IDENTIFICATION AS CONTROLLED FOREIGN COMPANY

(A) Basic identification rules [*ICTA 1988, ss 747, 750, 755D, Sch 24; FA 1993, s 119; FA 2000, s 104, Sch 31; FA 2002, ss 89, 90*]

CC Co, an unquoted company, is incorporated and resident in Blueland and carries on business there as a wholesaler. It obtains the majority of its goods from associated companies although 10% is obtained from local suppliers. The goods are exported to UK customers — the major one of which is ADE Co Ltd. CC Co has a share capital of 1,000 ordinary shares which are owned as follows

SS Co Ltd (non-UK resident company)	50
ADE Co Ltd (UK incorporated and resident company)	150
John James (UK domiciled and resident individual)	300
Mrs James (wife of John James)	300
Caroline James (daughter of Mr & Mrs James) living in France	200
	1,000

The shareholders of SS Co Ltd are all non-UK residents. The shareholders of ADE Co Ltd are Mr & Mrs Andrew James (parents of John James).

The following figures (converted into sterling) have been obtained for CC Co for the year to 30 April 2006.

	£
Profit before tax	7,000,000
Depreciation	1,000,000
Dividend proposed for year	500,000
Blueland tax paid on profits of year	1,200,000
Market value of plant and machinery at 1.5.05	2,500,000
Additions to plant and machinery in year	1,800,000
Original cost of industrial buildings (acquired prior to 1.5.05)	1,500,000

There were no disposals of fixed assets during the year.

The company is not a CFC with respect to any earlier accounting period.

CC is a controlled foreign company because

(i)   it is resident outside the UK

(ii)   it is controlled by persons resident in the UK, as follows

	UK residents Ordinary shares	Non-UK residents Ordinary shares
ADE Co Ltd	150	
John James	300	
Mrs James	300	
SS Co Ltd		50
Caroline James		200
	750	250
Percentage holding	75%	25%

(iii)   it is subject to a lower level of taxation in the country where it is resident

Notional UK chargeable profits	
Year ended 30 April 2006	£
Profit before tax	7,000,000
Add Depreciation	1,000,000
	8,000,000
Capital allowances (note (*c*))	1,135,000
	£6,865,000
£6,865,000 @ 30%	£2,059,500
75% thereof	£1,544,625
Overseas tax paid	£1,200,000

The overseas tax paid is less than three-quarters of the 'corresponding UK tax' so the company is regarded as being subject to a lower level of taxation (note (*b*)).

Notes

(*a*)   To be a controlled foreign company a company must be
   (i)   resident outside the UK
   (ii)   controlled by persons resident in the UK
   (iii)   subject to a 'lower level of taxation' in the territory in which it is resident.
   [*ICTA 1988, ss 747, 755D*].

(*b*)   The condition at (*a*)(iii) above is satisfied if the tax paid in the country in which the company is resident is less than three-quarters of the 'corresponding UK tax'. [*ICTA 1988, s 750; FA 1993, s 119(1)*].

(*c*)   **Capital allowances**

Plant and machinery	Main pool	Allowances
	£	£
Market value at 1.5.05	2,500,000	
Additions	1,800,000	
	4,300,000	
WDA (25%)	(1,075,000)	1,075,000
WDV c/f	£3,225,000	

Industrial buildings allowance
Original cost of building = £1,500,000

WDA £1,500,000 at 4%		60,000
Total allowances		£1,135,000

[*ICTA 1988, Sch 24 para 10; CAA 2001, Sch 2 para 66*].

106.1 Controlled Foreign Companies

(B) Effect of operation in second overseas territory [*ICTA 1988, ss 416, 747, 749, 750, 755, 756, Sch 24; FA 1993, s 119; FA 2000, s 104, Sch 31; FA 2002, ss 89, 90*]

FC Co is an unquoted company incorporated and resident in Redland where tax is levied at 20% and carries on business there as an importer/exporter. The majority of goods are exported to UK customers.

FC Co also has a presence in Whiteland where the tax rate is 30%. There is no double tax treaty in existence between Whiteland and Redland and the Whiteland authorities have ruled that the presence in Whiteland constitutes a permanent establishment. Redland gives unilateral double taxation relief in the same way as the UK. The following figures (converted into sterling) have been obtained for FC Co for the year to 30 September 2006.

	Whiteland £	Redland £	Total £
Profit before tax	40,000,000	50,000,000	90,000,000
Depreciation	—	6,000,000	6,000,000
Local tax paid on profits for year	12,000,000	10,000,000	22,000,000
Market value of plant and machinery at 1.10.05			24,000,000
Additions to fixed assets — plant and machinery			12,000,000

There were no disposals of fixed assets during the year.

FC Co has a share capital of 1,000 ordinary shares (registered) and 1,000 bearer shares which are owned as follows

	Ordinary shares	Bearer shares
TT Co Ltd (non-resident company)	50	
BDE Co Ltd (UK incorporated and resident company)	250	
XY Co (Blackland subsidiary of OY Co)	50	
Roger Brown (UK domiciled and resident individual)	300	
OY Co (incorporated and resident in Purpleland)	100	500
Will Rodgers (resident in Yellowland)		500
ACD Co (Orangeland incorporated and resident company)	250	
	1,000	1,000

The bearer shares have rights only to dividends (i.e. no voting rights).

The shares of BDE Co Ltd are owned by ACD Co. The shareholders of ACD Co are Orangeland residents.

OY Co purchased the shares in FC Co on 1 June 2006 from XZ Co Ltd — a UK incorporated and resident company — which had held the shares in FC Co for the previous three years. XZ Co Ltd is owned by UK residents.

FC is a controlled foreign company because

(i)   it is resident outside the UK
(ii) it is controlled by UK residents. The Revenue may ignore the bearer shares as they have no voting rights. The ordinary shares are held as follows

	UK residents Ordinary shares	Non-UK residents Ordinary shares
TT Co Ltd		50
BDE Co Ltd	250	
XY Co		50
Roger Brown	300	
OY Co		100
ACD Co		250
	550	450
Percentage holding	55%	45%

(iii) it is subject to a lower level of taxation in the country where it is resident

Notional UK chargeable profits
Year ended 30 September 2006

	£
Profit before tax	90,000,000
Add Depreciation	6,000,000
	96,000,000
Capital allowances (note (*a*))	9,000,000
	£87,000,000
£87,000,000 @ 30%	26,100,000
Less Double tax relief (Whiteland tax)	12,000,000
	£14,100,000
75% thereof	£10,575,000
Overseas tax paid (note (*b*))	£10,000,000

£10,000,000 is less than £10,575,000 so the company is regarded as being subject to a lower level of taxation. [*ICTA 1988, s 750; FA 1993, s 119(1)*].

Notes

(*a*) **Capital allowances** (plant and machinery)

	Main pool £	Total allowances £
Market value at 1.10.05	24,000,000	
Additions	12,000,000	
	36,000,000	
WDA 25%	9,000,000	9,000,000
WDV c/f	£27,000,000	

106.2 Controlled Foreign Companies

(b) **Overseas tax paid**
     Whiteland
     Profit before tax   £40,000,000

     Whiteland tax at 30%   £12,000,000

Redland	Whiteland	Redland	Total
Profit before tax	£40,000,000	£50,000,000	£90,000,000
Redland tax at 20%	8,000,000	10,000,000	18,000,000
Less credit for Whiteland tax			
(restricted to 20%)	(8,000,000)		(8,000,000)
Tax in Redland	—	£10,000,000	£10,000,000

The overseas tax brought into the CFC calculation is that paid in the country of residence. Therefore even though the total tax paid during the year was £22,000,000 only the £10,000,000 paid in Redland is taken into account.

106.2 **APPORTIONMENT OF PROFITS** [*ICTA 1988, s 752*]

(A)
In 106.1(A) above CC Co's notional UK chargeable profits and creditable tax are apportioned among the persons who had an interest in the company during its accounting period.

Shareholder	% shareholding	Attributable profits £	Creditable tax £
SS Co Ltd	5	343,250	60,000
ADE Co Ltd	15	1,029,750	180,000
John James	30	2,059,500	360,000
Mrs James	30	2,059,500	360,000
Caroline James	20	1,373,000	240,000
	100%	£6,865,000	£1,200,000

ADE Co Ltd is the only UK resident company to which chargeable profits and creditable tax are apportioned. ADE Co Ltd is chargeable to corporation tax on a sum equal to the profits of CC Co which are apportioned to it, and this corporation tax charge is then reduced by the apportioned amount of creditable tax. The corporation tax rate applicable is the rate (or average rate) applicable to ADE Co Ltd's own profits for the accounting period in which CC Co's accounting period ends. ADE Co Ltd has a 30 April year end.

ADE Co Ltd

Year to 30 April 2006

Tax computations — before apportionment

	£
Schedule D, Case I	8,000,000
Losses brought forward	—
	8,000,000
Schedule D, Case III	50,000
Schedule D, Case V	1,250,000
Chargeable gains	250,000
	£9,550,000
UK tax at 30%	2,865,000
DTR on Schedule D, Case V income	(412,500)
CT liability	£2,452,500

Tax computations — after apportionment

Schedule D, Case I	8,000,000
Losses brought forward	—
	8,000,000
Schedule D, Case III	50,000
Schedule D, Case V	1,250,000
Chargeable gains	250,000
CFC apportionment	1,029,750
	£10,579,750
UK tax at 30%	3,173,925
DTR on Schedule D, Case V income	(412,500)
CFC creditable tax	(180,000)
CT liability	£2,581,425
Additional tax	£128,925

Note

(a) No charge arises unless at least 25% of the CFC's chargeable profits for the period is apportioned either to the UK resident company or to persons connected or associated with it.

(B)

In 106.1(B) above both BDE Co Ltd and XZ Co Ltd will be chargeable to corporation tax on the profits of FC Co apportionable to them. XZ Co Ltd is liable because it owned shares in FC Co at some time during the year to 30 September 2006 (even though it had disposed of its shareholding before that date). XZ Co Ltd should apportion such proportion of the profits as is attributable to the period to 31 May 2006.

106.3   Controlled Foreign Companies

106.3 **ACCEPTABLE DISTRIBUTION POLICY** [*ICTA 1988, s 748, Sch 25 Pt 1; FA 1994, s 134; FA 1996, s 182, Sch 36 para 4; FA 2001, s 82*]

DEF Co Ltd, a UK incorporated and resident company with two associated companies, holds 35% of the shares of LNB Co, an unquoted controlled foreign company resident in Pinkland, where tax is levied at only 10%.

LNB Co has chargeable profits for the year ended 31 March 2006 of £500,000. No withholding tax is applicable in Pinkland.

The following information is available in respect of DEF.

Year to 31 March	2006	2007
	£	£
Schedule D, Case I profit	600,000	780,000
Schedule D, Case III income	10,000	10,000
Chargeable gains	90,000	—
Schedule D, Case V income (gross) (tax suffered £30,000)	100,000	—

LNB Co

Calculation of profits apportioned to DEF Co Ltd and dividend required to avoid apportionment

	£
Chargeable profits for the year ended 31 March 2006	500,000
Deduct creditable tax	50,000
Net chargeable profits	£450,000
Amount of distribution required to avoid apportionment 90% × £450,000	£405,000

	Apportionment of profit	Dividend
	£	£
DEF share		
35% × £500,000: 35% × £405,000	175,000	141,750
Creditable underlying tax	17,500	15,750
		£157,500

DEF Co Ltd — With apportionment

Year to 31 March	2006	2007
	£	£
Schedule D, Case I	600,000	780,000
Schedule D, Case III	10,000	10,000
Chargeable gains	90,000	—
Schedule D, Case V income	100,000	—
CFC apportionment	175,000	—
	£975,000	£790,000

	£	2006 £	2007 £
UK tax thereon at 30%		292,500	237,000
Less			
DTR on Case V income	(30,000)		
CFC creditable tax	(17,500)	(47,500)	
Mainstream tax payable		£245,000	£237,000

DEF Co Ltd — If dividend paid in y/e 31.3.07

Year to 31 March

	2006 £	2007 £
Schedule D, Case I	600,000	780,000
Schedule D, Case III	10,000	10,000
Chargeable gains	90,000	—
Schedule D, Case V income	100,000	157,500
	£800,000	£947,500
UK tax thereon at 30%	240,000	284,250
Less		
DTR	(30,000)	(15,750)
Mainstream tax payable	£210,000	£268,500
Tax saving (cost)	£35,000	£(31,500)

DEF Co Ltd will make a net tax saving of £3,500 in tax if LBN Co pays the required dividend for the year ended 31 March 2006 by 31 March 2007 (see note (*b*)).

Notes

(*a*) If a controlled foreign company pursues an acceptable distribution policy in respect of an accounting period, no apportionment is made.

(*b*) The controlled foreign company has, in fact, 18 months after the end of the accounting period in which to pay the dividend, so, in this example, payment at any time before 1 October 2007 would have satisfied the 'acceptable distribution policy' test. The Board may allow longer than 18 months in any particular case. [*ICTA 1988, Sch 25 para 2(1)(b); FA 1994, s 134(2)(a)*].

106.4   Controlled Foreign Companies

106.4 **SUBSEQUENT DIVIDEND** [*ICTA 1988, s 754(5), Sch 26 para 4(1)–(3); FA 1998, Sch 17 para 36*]

JF Co is a CFC in respect of the year ended 31 March 2005. In consequence an apportionment of its profit for that year (£900,000) has been made and KLM Ltd, a UK incorporated and resident company with a $\frac{1}{3}$ interest in JF Co, has been apportioned chargeable profits of £300,000 (gross). Creditable tax attributed to KLM is £30,000.

On 1 November 2006 JF Co paid a dividend of £528,000 in respect of the year ended 31 March 2005 of which KLM Ltd's share was £176,000. There is no withholding tax and the underlying tax rate is 12%.

In the subsequent years ended 31 March 2006 and 2007, JF Co made profits of only £15,000 and £45,000.

The corporation tax computations for KLM Ltd show that in the three years ended 31 March 2007 its Schedule D, Case I profits were £250,000, £300,000 and £450,000 respectively. Schedule D, Case III income for the three years was £10,000 per annum. For the year ended 31 March 2006 there were chargeable gains of £16,000 and charges on income of £8,000. Small companies rate does not apply, because there are several associated companies.

KLM Ltd

Tax computations

Year to 31 March	2005	2006	2007
	£	£	£
Schedule D, Case I profits	250,000	300,000	450,000
Schedule D, Case III income	10,000	10,000	10,000
Chargeable gains	—	16,000	
CFC apportionment	300,000	—	—
Schedule D, Case V income (£176,000 grossed up at 12%)	—	—	200,000
	560,000	326,000	660,000
Charges on income		(8,000)	
	£560,000	£318,000	£660,000
Tax at 30%	168,000	95,400	198,000
CFC creditable tax	(30,000)		
DTR on dividend (£200,000 at 12%)			(24,000)
Credit for UK tax on apportionment (note (*a*))			(40,000)
	£138,000	£95,400	£134,000

Notes   £

(a) Tax on CFC apportionment — £300,000 × 30%   90,000
     CFC creditable tax   (30,000)

     Net tax suffered   £60,000

     Actual dividend (gross) — £200,000

     Credit for UK tax on apportionment $\left(\dfrac{200,000}{300,000}\right)$ × £60,000   £40,000

(b) A CFC is exempted from apportionment for an accounting period if it makes an acceptable distribution within 18 months of the end of that period. Thus, had the dividend been paid by 30 September 2006, no apportionment need have been made. A CFC is also exempted from apportionment if its chargeable profits for the period do not exceed £50,000.

(c) The CFC legislation applies automatically where all the necessary conditions are met. UK companies are thus required to include significant interests in CFCs in their tax returns and to self-assess any CFC tax due.

107   Corporate Venturing Scheme

107.1 **INVESTMENT RELIEF** [*FA 2000, Sch 15 paras 39–66*]

(A) General

A Ltd draws up accounts each year to 31 December. In the year ended 31 December 2006, A Ltd subscribes for 10,000 shares in B Ltd, costing £80,000, and for 5,000 shares in C Ltd, costing £50,000. A Ltd holds no other shares in either company and both investments qualify for investment relief under the corporate venturing scheme. A Ltd's only income or gains for the year ended 31 December 2006 are trading profits of £75,000 and net Schedule D, Case III income of £500.

A Ltd's corporation tax computation for the year ended 31 December 2006 is as follows

	£	£
Schedule D, Case I		75,000
Schedule D, Case III		500
Profits		75,500
Corporation tax @ 19%		14,345
Less CVS investment relief £130,000 @		14,345
20% = £26,000 but restricted to		
CT due		Nil

CVS investment relief is attributable to the shares as follows

B Ltd shares $\dfrac{80,000}{80,000 + 50,000} \times £14,345 = £8,828$

C Ltd shares $\dfrac{50,000}{80,000 + 50,000} \times £14,345 = £5,517$

Notes

(*a*) Investment relief cannot be claimed until the issuing company or its subsidiary has carried on the funded trade (i.e. the trade in which the funds raised by the issue of shares are to be used) for four months. The issuing company must also have issued the investing company with a compliance certificate in respect of the shares concerned. Subject to this, a claim for investment relief must be made within six years of the end of the accounting period to which the relief relates. [*FA 1998, Sch 18 para 55; FA 2000, Sch 15 para 40*].

(*b*) Investment relief is given as a reduction in the corporation tax liability equal to 20% of the aggregate amount subscribed or, if less, the amount which reduces the liability to nil. [*FA 2000, Sch 15 para 39*]. Where the investing company subscribes for two or more issues of shares in an accounting period, relief is attributed to shares in the same proportions as the amount subscribed for each issue. [*FA 2000, Sch 15 para 45(1)(2)*].

(B) Withdrawal of investment relief

In October 2008, A Ltd, the company in (A) above, sells all of the shares in B Ltd which it had subscribed for at arm's length for the market value of (i) £100,000 or (ii) £45,000.

CVS investment relief is withdrawn as follows

(i) Proceeds £100,000

	£
Relief attributed to shares sold (see (A) above)	8,828
Consideration received £100,000 × $\left(\dfrac{8,828}{80,000 \times 20\%}\right)$ × 20%	11,035
Excess of 20% of the adjusted consideration over relief	£2,207
Relief withdrawn: Schedule D, Case VI for y/e 31.12.06	£8,828

(ii) Proceeds £45,000

	£
Relief attributed to shares sold	8,828
Consideration received £45,000 × $\left(\dfrac{8,828}{80,000 \times 20\%}\right)$ × 20%	4,965
Excess of relief over 20% of the adjusted consideration	£3,863
Relief withdrawn: Schedule D, Case VI for y/e 31.12.06	£4,965

Notes

(*a*) Investment relief is withdrawn or reduced on the sale of the shares within the qualification period (i.e. the period ending three years after the issue of the shares or, if later and where relevant, three years after the commencement of the trade by the issuing company or its subsidiary). If the relief attributable to the shares is greater than 20% of the proceeds, the relief is reduced by the smaller of those amounts, as in (ii). Otherwise, the relief is withdrawn in full as in (i). Where the relief given was restricted to less than 20% of the amount subscribed, as in this case, the proceeds are adjusted by multiplying them by the amount of the relief divided by 20% of the amount subscribed. [*FA 2000, Sch 15 paras 46, 96*].

(*b*) Relief is, in any event, withdrawn in full if the disposal is not at arm's length for full consideration, by way of a distribution in the course of dissolving or winding up the issuing company, or a disposal within *TCGA 1992, s 24(1)* (entire loss, destruction etc.) or *s 24(2)* (negligible value). [*FA 2000, Sch 15 para 46(2)*].

(*c*) Investment relief is also withdrawn or reduced if the investing company (or a connected person) receives significant value from the issuing company (or connected person) during the restriction period (i.e. the period beginning one year before the issue of the shares and ending at the end of the qualification period); if the issuing company (or its subsidiary) repays, redeems or repurchases its share capital or makes a payment to a shareholder for giving up rights to the share capital during the restriction period, or an option is granted over the relevant shares during the qualification period. [*FA 2000, Sch 15 paras 47–59; FA 2001, Sch 16 paras 6–9*].

107.2 Corporate Venturing Scheme

107.2 **LOSS RELIEF** [*FA 2000, Sch 15 paras 67–72, 94*]

X Ltd draws up accounts each year to 31 December. The company subscribes for 50,000 shares in Y Ltd for £50,000 in July 2006. Y Ltd commences to trade at that time. The investment qualifies for corporate venturing scheme investment relief of £10,000 which X Ltd is able to claim in full. It sells the shares in July 2011 for £20,000, having held the shares continuously since July 2006. X Ltd's trading profits for the year ended 31 December 2011 are £12,000, and those for the year ended 31 December 2010 are £6,000. The company has no other income or chargeable gains for either year.

X Ltd may claim relief for its loss on the Y Ltd shares as follows:

	£	£
Disposal proceeds		20,000
Deduct acquisition cost	50,000	
Less investment relief	10,000	40,000
Allowable loss		£20,000

£12,000 of the loss may be set off against the income of the year ended 31 December 2011, and £6,000 against the income of the year ended 31 December 2010. The balance of the loss (£2,000) is carried forward to the year ended 31 December 2012 as a capital loss, relievable against chargeable gains only.

Notes

(*a*)   A claim to set off a loss on shares to which investment relief is attributable (and not wholly withdrawn as a result of the disposal) against income of the accounting period in which it is incurred and of the preceding twelve months must be made within two years of the end of the accounting period of loss. [*FA 2000, Sch 15 para 68(2)*].

(*b*)   The investment relief is not withdrawn on the disposal of the shares in Y Ltd as X Ltd has held the shares throughout the qualification period ending three years after the issue of the shares (or the date of the commencement of the issuing company's trade, if later). [*FA 2000, Sch 15 paras 3, 46*].

107.3 **DEFERRAL RELIEF** [*FA 2000, Sch 15 paras 73–79*]

(A) Relief available

Z Ltd, which makes up accounts to 31 March each year, sells its shares in F Ltd (to which CVS investment relief is attributable) in January 2009, realising a chargeable gain of £100,000. Z Ltd makes the following investments in shares, all of which qualify for CVS investment relief:

(i)   10,000 shares in K Ltd for £10,000 in July 2008;

(ii)   10,000 shares in L Ltd for £50,000 in February 2009;

(iii) 25,000 shares in M Ltd for £50,000 in January 2010;

(iv)   10,000 shares in S Ltd for £100,000 in January 2012.

Z Ltd can claim up to a total amount of £100,000 in deferral relief in respect of the gain on the F Ltd shares by setting corresponding amounts of expenditure on the share issues in (i), (ii) or (iii) against it. It need not defer the gain against the earliest acquisition, so it can claim to defer the full amount of the gain against (ii) and (iii) only if it wishes.

Z Ltd cannot defer any of the gain against (iv) because the S Ltd shares are not issued in the period beginning one year before and ending three years after the chargeable gain accrued.

Notes

(*a*) There is no specific time limit for a deferral relief claim. Accordingly, the time limit is six years from the end of the accounting period in which the new investment is made. [*FA 1988, Sch 18 para 55*].

(*b*) Deferral relief can only be claimed in respect of a chargeable gain on shares to which CVS investment relief is attributable (and which is not wholly withdrawn as a result of the disposal), or on a gain arising from a chargeable event under these provisions (see (B) below). [*FA 2000, Sch 15 para 73*].

107.3   Corporate Venturing Scheme

(B) Chargeable event

Z Ltd, the company in (A) above, defers its gain on the disposal of the B Ltd shares against the shares in K Ltd (£10,000), L Ltd (£50,000) and M Ltd (£40,000) acquired as in (i), (ii) and (iii) in (A) above. Z Ltd sells half of the shares in M Ltd in March 2010 for £35,000, which is its only disposal of assets in the year ended 31 March 2010.

Z Ltd's chargeable gains for the year ended 31 March 2010 are

M Ltd shares

	£
Disposal proceeds	35,000
Less acquisition cost £50,000 × $\frac{1}{2}$	25,000
Unindexed gain	10,000
Less indexation £25,000 @ say 10%	2,500
Chargeable gain	£7,500

B Ltd shares

Deferred gain revived £40,000 × $\frac{1}{2}$	£20,000
Taxable gains y/e 31.3.10 (£7,500 + £20,000)	£27,500

Notes

(*a*)   A chargeable event occurs when the company disposes of the replacement shares or on the occurrence of any other event that causes the investment relief attributable to those shares to be withdrawn if that event occurs after the gain which is to be deferred accrues. [*FA 2000, Sch 15 para 78(1)(2)*].

(*b*)   On the happening of the first chargeable event in relation to the replacement shares, the company is treated at that time as making a chargeable gain equal to the deferred gain that was attributed to those shares. [*FA 2000, Sch 15 para 79*].

(*c*)   Z Ltd could claim to defer the gains on both the M Ltd and B Ltd shares against the subscription of shares in S Ltd in January 2012 (see (A) above).

108   Double Tax Relief

108.1 MEASURE OF RELIEF

(A) Relief for withholding tax [*ICTA 1988, ss 790(4)–(6), 795, 797*]

A Ltd owns 5% of the share capital of B Ltd, a company resident in an overseas country which has no double taxation agreement with the UK. The following facts relate to A Ltd's accounting period for the year ended 31 March 2007.

	£
Trading profits	1,500,000
Dividend from B Ltd (£80,000 less withholding tax £20,000)	60,000

A Ltd's tax liability is

	Schedule D Case I	Schedule D Case V	Total
	£	£	£
Profits	1,500,000	80,000	1,580,000
CT at 30%	450,000	24,000	474,800
Relief for foreign tax (note (*a*))	—	(20,000)	(20,000)
	£450,000	£4,000	£454,000

Note

(*a*)   Because the shareholding in B Ltd is less than 10%, no credit is available for the underlying foreign tax on B Ltd's profits. Credit is available for withholding tax.

108.1 Double Tax Relief

(B) Relief for underlying tax [*ICTA 1988, ss 790(6), 795, 797, 799, 806A–806J; FA 2000, s 103, Sch 30; FA 2001, Sch 27*]

H Ltd, a UK resident company, which prepares accounts to 31 March each year, owns 40% of the share capital and voting power of S Ltd, a company resident abroad. On 3 May 2006 H Ltd received a dividend of £70,000 from S Ltd which had suffered withholding tax at 30%. The dividend was paid out of the profits for the year ended 30 June 2006. The following is an extract from the profit and loss account of S Ltd for that year.

	£	£
Profit before tax		900,000
Tax on profits	250,000	
Deferred tax	150,000	400,000
Profit after tax		£500,000

H Ltd may obtain relief in its year ended 31 March 2007 as follows

	£	£
Dividend received		70,000
Add Withholding tax		30,000
		100,000
Add Underlying tax at $33\frac{1}{3}$% (note (*a*))		50,000
		£150,000
UK Corporation tax at 30%		45,000
Overseas tax suffered		
Withholding tax	30,000	
Creditable underlying tax (£150,000 × 30%)	45,000	
	75,000	
Limited to UK tax	45,000	(45,000)
Overseas taxation unrelieved (£30,000 + £50,000 − £45,000) (note (*b*))	£35,000	

Notes

(*a*) Rate of underlying tax $= \dfrac{\text{actual tax paid} \times 100}{\text{actual tax paid} + \text{relevant profit}}$

$$= \frac{250,000 \times 100}{250,000 + 500,000}$$

$$= 33\tfrac{1}{3}\%$$

(*b*) For dividends paid on or after 31 March 2001, further relief is available for otherwise unrelieved withholding and underlying tax to the extent that it is eligible unrelieved foreign tax (EUFT). Broadly, EUFT is limited to a maximum of 45% of the gross dividend less the double tax relief offset. In this example, the EUFT is £27,500, including Case A EUFT of £22,500 (£150,000 @ 45% = £67,500 less tax credited of £45,000) and Case B EUFT of £5,000 (underlying tax of £50,000 less tax credited of £45,000), Case A being all withholding tax and Case B underlying tax. See 108.4 below.

(c)   EUFT can be used to offset the UK tax on any qualifying foreign dividends (if any) of the same period ('onshore pooling'). Alternatively, it can be carried backwards for three years (but not before 31 March 2001) or carried forward indefinitely, to be set against the UK tax payable on dividends from the same source in other periods. A company can surrender EUFT to another company in the same group. See 108.3 below.

108.2 **ALLOCATION OF CHARGES ETC.** [*ICTA 1988, ss 790(6), 795, 797, 799*]
The following information about A Ltd (which owns 20% of the voting power of B Ltd, a non-resident company) for the year ended 31 March 2007 is relevant.

	£
UK income	1,200,000
UK chargeable gains	300,000
Overseas income (tax rate 40%) from B Ltd (gross)	300,000
Charges paid (qualifying charitable donations)	150,000

A Ltd may allocate charges as it wishes in order to obtain maximum double tax relief. The following calculation shows how this is best done

	UK income and gains £	Overseas income £	Total £
Income and gains	1,500,000	300,000	1,800,000
Deduct Charges (note (*a*))	150,000	—	150,000
	£1,350,000	£300,000	£1,650,000
CT at 30%	405,000	90,000	495,000
Deduct Double tax relief (note (*b*))	—	(90,000)	(90,000)
CT liability	£405,000	—	£405,000

Notes
(a)   To obtain the best advantage, charges should be set off firstly against UK income and gains and then against overseas income. If there is more than one overseas income source, the charges should be set as far as possible against income subject to a lower rather than a higher rate of overseas tax. (See also note (*e*) below.)

(b)   Double tax relief is the lower of

(i)   Overseas tax suffered, 40% × £300,000   £120,000

and

(ii)   CT liability on overseas income   £93,000

Therefore, double tax relief is   £93,000

(c) If charges were set off against overseas income first, the following tax would be payable

	UK income and gains £	Overseas income £	Total £
Income and gains	1,500,000	300,000	1,800,000
Deduct Charges	—	150,000	150,000
	£1,500,000	£150,000	£1,650,000
CT at 30%	450,000	45,000	495,000
Deduct Double tax relief	—	(45,000)	(45,000)
CT liability	£450,000	—	£450,000

This gives a maximum double tax relief of £45,000. Compared with the recommended allocation, £45,000 of double tax relief (£90,000 – £45,000) is lost (but see note (d) below).

(d) Where the foreign tax cannot be relieved in the current accounting period it can be carried backwards for three years or carried forward indefinitely, to be set against the UK tax payable on dividends of the permitted type in other periods [*ICTA 1988, s 806E*]. In addition, a company can surrender foreign tax to another company in the same group [*ICTA 1988, s 806H*]. See 108.1(B) above.

108.3 **MIXING** [*ICTA 1988, s 799(1)(b)(1A)(1B), s 801*]

(A) Simple mixer company
UK plc wholly owns Dutch Holding BV which in turn wholly owns Low Tax Co which pays tax at 10% and High Tax Co which pays tax at 40%. Both subsidiaries make pre-tax profits of £100 and make full distributions to the UK via Dutch Holding BV which does not pay any tax on the dividends. The tax position for UK plc is as follows.

	£
Net dividend	150
Underlying tax	50
Schedule D Case V	200
Corporation tax @ 30%	60
Double tax relief (note (a))	(40)
UK tax liability	£20
Unused tax credits	£10

Notes
(a) Claims for credit relief made on or after 31 March 2001 are restricted by provisions which effectively eliminate the tax advantage of routing overseas dividends through

'mixer' companies in favourable foreign jurisdictions (such as the Netherlands). The relievable underlying tax in respect of any dividend paid up through an overseas subsidiary is restricted to the corporation tax rate in force at the time the dividend was paid, applied to the sum of the dividend and the underlying tax to be taken into account. Thus, full relief is available for tax of £10 paid by Low Tax Co but although High Tax Co suffers tax of £40, relief of only £30 is available due to the 'mixer cap' restriction.

(*b*)   The 'mixer cap' restriction does not apply where the overseas companies paying and receiving the dividend are 'related' and resident in the same overseas territory. It is assumed in this example and the examples below that the companies concerned are each resident in different countries.

(*c*)   It is assumed for the purpose of this example and the example below that the companies resident in low-tax jurisdictions are all trading companies which are exempt from the CFC rules otherwise than through pursuing an acceptable distribution policy. Thus the provisions in *ICTA 1988, s 801C* for the separate streaming of the dividend for credit relief purposes would not apply.

(B) Chain of subsidiaries—high into low tax mixing

UK plc wholly owns Low Tax Co which pays tax at 20% and which in turn wholly owns High Tax Co which pays tax at 40%. Both subsidiaries make pre-tax profits of £100 and make full distributions. The dividend from High Tax Co is exempt from tax in the hands of Low Tax Co. The tax position for UK plc is as follows.

	£
Net dividend	140
Underlying tax	60
Schedule D Case V	200
Corporation tax @ 30%	60
Double tax relief (note (*a*))	(50)
UK tax liability	£10
Unused tax credits	£10

Notes

(*a*)   Credit relief is fully available Low Tax Co of £20 but the tax paid by High Tax Co £40 is restricted to £30 by the mixer cap (see note (*a*) at (A) above).

(*b*)   See also notes (*a*) to (*c*) at (A) above.

108.4 Double Tax Relief

(C) Chain of subsidiaries—low into high tax mixing

UK plc wholly owns High Tax Co which pays tax at 40% and which in turn wholly owns Low Tax Co which pays tax at 20%. Both subsidiaries make pre-tax profits of £100 and make full distributions. The dividend from Low Tax Co is exempt from tax in the hands of High Tax Co. The tax position for UK plc is as follows.

	£
Net dividend	140
Underlying tax	60
Schedule D Case V	200
Corporation tax @ 30%	60
Double tax relief (note (a))	(60)
UK tax liability	—

Notes

(a) The mixer cap restriction does not apply to the dividend paid by Low Tax Co to High Tax Co because the tax paid of £20 is lower than 30% of the sum of the dividend (£80) and the underlying tax (£20). Equally, the mixer cap restriction does not apply to the dividend paid by High Tax Co to UK plc because the total tax paid of £60 (£20 + £40) is no higher than 30% of the sum of the dividend of £140 (£80 + £60) and the underlying tax of £60 (£20 + £40).

(b) See also notes (a) to (c) at (A) above.

108.4 ONSHORE POOLING AND UTILISATION OF ELIGIBLE UNRELIEVED FOREIGN TAX [ICTA 1988, ss 806A–806J, 826(7BB)(7BC)]

(A) Pooling

UK plc has two wholly owned foreign subsidiaries, High Tax Co which pays tax at 40% and Low Tax Co which pays tax at 10%. The dividend from High Tax Co is subject to withholding tax of £3. Both subsidiaries make pre-tax profits of £100 and make full distributions to the UK.

	High Tax Co	Low Tax Co	Pool
	£	£	£
Gross dividend (including withholding tax)	60	90	150
Underlying tax	40	10	50
Schedule D Case V	100	100	200
Corporation tax @ 30%	30	30	60
Double tax relief (note (b))	(30)	(10)	(40)
UK tax liability	—	20	20
Case B EUFT (note (a))	10		(10)
Case A EUFT (note (a))	3		(3)
Net liability			£7

Notes

(a) A partial relief from the capping restriction (see examples in 108.3 above) is provided by a system of 'onshore pooling' of certain foreign dividends, against the tax on which may be set the excess tax over the cap, allowing relief up to a maximum of 45% in total. Relief may similarly be obtained up to the same overall 45% limit for unrelieved withholding and underlying tax on dividends received directly from overseas subsidiaries.

The scheme provides for the set-off of *'eligible unrelieved foreign tax'* against the UK tax arising on *'qualifying foreign dividends'*.

Eligible unrelieved foreign tax (EUFT) is the excess, subject to the 45% maximum limit, of:

(i) the credit for the foreign tax, excluding any underlying tax which has been restricted by the 30% cap, of a foreign dividend over the UK tax charged on the dividend (this being referred to as 'Case A' EUFT); and

(ii) the underlying tax of a foreign dividend which has been restricted by the mixer cap (this being referred to as 'Case B' EUFT).

Qualifying foreign dividends (QFDs) are foreign dividends other than dividends paid by controlled foreign companies to satisfy the acceptable distribution policy test (see below), or dividends representing such dividends, and dividends for which relief is itself restricted (and so gives rise to EUFT) (as above).

(b) High Tax Co suffers underlying tax of £40 and withholding tax of £3, which is restricted by the mixer cap, giving rise to Case B EUFT of £10 and Case A EUFT of £3. Low Tax Co suffers underlying tax of £10, leaving a UK tax liability of £20. This can be relieved by the EUFT of £13 leaving a net liability of £7. Had High Tax Co been subject to tax at 50%, the Case B EUFT would have been restricted to £15 (maximum relievable tax at 45% (£45) less the underlying tax as restricted by the mixer cap at 30% (£30)), leaving £5 of foreign tax which could not be used, and a net UK tax liability of £2.

(c) See also notes (a) to (c) in Example at (A) above.

(B) 'Tainted' dividends
UK plc wholly owns Dutch Holding BV which in turn wholly owns High Tax Co A which pays tax at 40% and Low Tax Co which pays tax at 10%. UK plc also wholly owns High Tax Co B which pays tax at 50%. All the subsidiaries make pre-tax profits of £100 and make full distributions (High Tax Co A and Low Tax Co via Dutch Holding BV).

	Dutch Holding BV £	High Tax Co B £	Total £
Net dividend	150	50	200
Underlying tax	50	50	100
Schedule D Case V	200	100	300
Corporation tax @ 30%	60	30	90
Double tax relief (note (a))	(40)	(30)	(70)
UK tax liability	£20	—	£20
Unused Case B EUFT (note (a))	£10	£15	

108.4 Double Tax Relief

Notes

(a) High Tax Co A suffers underlying tax of £40 which is restricted by the 30% mixer cap giving rise to Case B EUFT of £10. The dividend paid up to UK plc is a blend of this capped dividend and the 10% taxed dividend from Low Tax Co. Since EUFT has arisen on it, the dividend is not a 'qualifying foreign dividend' and so does not qualify for onshore pooling. UK tax of £20 arises (after relief for the underlying tax) on the Low Tax Co element of the blended dividend but the Case B EUFT of £10 cannot be relieved against it and can only be carried back or carried forward (assuming there is no other UK tax liability on low taxed dividends against which it could be relieved).

High Tax Co B suffers underlying tax of £50 which is restricted by the 30% mixer cap giving rise to Case B EUFT of £15 (limited by the 45% cap). Since the blended dividend from Dutch Holding BV is not a 'qualifying foreign dividend' and cannot be pooled, the EUFT can only be carried back or carried forward, leaving a net UK tax liability of £20.

(b) See also note (a) to (A) above and notes (a) to (c) at 108.3(A) above.

(C) Excluding underlying tax from a claim to avoid 'tainting'

The position is as per (B) above but the claim to High Tax Co A's underlying tax to 30% is limited to allow for the blended dividend from Dutch Holding BV to be a 'qualifying foreign dividend' and thus to qualify for onshore pooling.

	Dutch Holding BV £	High Tax Co B £	Pool £
Net dividend	150	50	200
Underlying tax	50	50	100
Schedule D Case V	200	100	300
Corporation tax @ 30%	60	30	90
Double tax relief (as per limited claim)	(40)	(30)	(70)
UK tax liability	20	—	20
Case B EUFT (restricted to 45%)(note (b))	—	15	(15)
Net UK tax liability			£5

Notes

(a) The claim for relief may be so framed as to exclude any specified amounts of underlying tax from being taken into account for this purpose. This may prevent the application of the mixer cap in certain cases and so allow for onshore pooling (see (B) above).

(b) The UK tax of £20 can be relieved by the Case B EUFT of £15 suffered by High Tax Co B, leaving a net UK tax liability of £5. The Case B EUFT of £10 arising on the dividend from High Tax Co A is lost.

(c) See also note (a) to (A) above and notes (a) to (c) at 108.3(A) above.

109   Exchange Gains and Losses

[*FA 1993, ss 92–95, 125–170, Schs 15–18; FA 1994, ss 114–116; FA 1995, ss 130–132, Sch 24; FA 2002, ss 79, 81, Sch 23*]

109.1   TRADING EXCHANGE GAINS AND LOSSES — GENERAL

Tinman plc, a UK trading company prepares its annual accounts to 31 March and sells goods on 4 December 2001 to a customer in the land of Oz for Oz $540,000. The customer pays Oz $140,000 on account on 1 February 2002 and the balance of Oz $400,000 remains outstanding on 31 March 2002. The exchange rates on the relevant dates are as follows

4 December 2001	£1 = 3 Oz $
1 February 2002	£1 = 2.9 Oz $
31 March 2002	£1 = 2.75 Oz $

The account can be summarised over the accrual period (4.12.01 to 31.3.02) as follows

Date	Amount	Exchange Rate	(Decrease)	£ equivalent
	Oz $	Oz /£	Oz $	
4.12.01	540,000	3.0	—	180,000
1.2.02	400,000	2.9	(140,000)	(48,276)
31.3.02	400,000	2.75	—	145,455

The exchange gain is calculated as follows

	£	£
Sterling equivalent 31.3.02		145,455
Less sterling equivalent 4.12.01	180,000	
Adjusted for decrease	(48,276)	131,724
Exchange gain		£13,731

The exchange gain falls to be included in Tinman plc's profits chargeable to corporation tax for the year ended 31 March 2002.

Notes

(*a*)   The *Finance Act 1993* foreign exchange gains and losses rules apply from a company's Commencement Day, being the first day of its first accounting period beginning on or after 23 March 1995 and to subsequent accounting periods beginning before 1 October 2002. There are transitional provisions for calculating exchange differences on transactions straddling the Commencement Day. These rules are repealed by *FA 2002* with effect for accounting periods beginning on or after 1 October 2002 and were largely reproduced and assimilated within the rules for loan relationships and derivative contracts. A number of original transitional provisions still apply and new transitional provisions apply to bring amounts into account in accounting periods beginning on or after 1 October 2002, either as debits or credits within the loan relationships rules or as chargeable gains or losses within *TCGA 1992.* [*FA 1993, s 165, Sch 16; FA 2002, ss 79, 81, Sch 23; SI 1994 No 3224; SI 2002 No 1969; SI 2002 No 1970*].

(*b*)   Under the *FA 1993* rules, where a qualifying asset (as in this example), qualifying liability or currency contract is held or owed solely for the purposes of a company's trade, an exchange gain is treated as a taxable receipt of the trade for the accounting period in which the accrual period falls. An exchange loss is treated as a deductible trading expense. [*FA 1993, s 128*]. Similar rules apply under the provisions operating for accounting periods beginning on or after 1 October 2002. Special rules (not illustrated here) apply to non-trading exchange gains and losses.

109.2   Exchange Gains and Losses

109.2 **DEFERRAL OF UNREALISED EXCHANGE GAINS** [*FA 1993, ss 139–143*]
On 1 October 2000, Tinkerbell plc, a UK trading company preparing accounts to 30 September, obtains a three-year loan of NNL $750,000 from its parent in Neverneverland to buy plant. For the years ended 30 September 2001 and 2002, the following information relating to Tinkerbell plc is relevant.

	At 1.10.00	At 30.9.01	At 30.9.02
Exchange rate NNL $ to £	1.5	1.6	1.69
Loan from parent (in £)	500,000	468,750	443,787

	Y/e 30.9.01 £	Y/e 30.9.02 £
Net exchange gains on qualifying advances, borrowings and currency contracts	36,000	18,000
Profits chargeable to CT (inclusive of net exchange gains)	150,000	275,000

Apart from the parent company loan, there were no other exchange gains or losses on long-term (one year or more) capital assets and liabilities.

The exchange gains available for deferral for the years ended 30 September 2001 and 2002 are calculated as follows

Y/e 30.9.01
Lower of
— unrealised exchange gains on long-term
  capital assets and liabilities
  £(500,000 − 468,750)   £31,250

— net exchange gains   £36,000

	£
Lower is	31,250
Less £150,000 @ 10%	15,000
Maximum deferral claim possible	£16,250

Profits chargeable to CT if maximum deferral claim made
£(150,000 − 16,250)   £133,750

Y/e 30.9.02 (assuming that maximum claim made for y/e 30.9.01)
Lower of
— unrealised exchange gains on long-term
  capital assets and liabilities
  £(468,750 − 443,787 + 16,250*)   £41,213

— net exchange gains £(18,000 + 16,250*)   £34,250

	£
Lower is	34,250
Less £(275,000 + 16,250*) = £291,250 @ 10%	29,125
Maximum deferral claim possible	£5,125
Profits chargeable to CT if maximum deferral claim made £(275,000 + 16,250* − 5,125)	£286,125

*   See note (*b*)

Notes

(*a*)   A company may claim to defer to the next accounting period all or part of an unrealised exchange gain on a long-term capital asset or liability, the maximum available to be deferred being calculated as above. Special rules (not illustrated here) apply to a member of a 75% group of companies.

(*b*)   The exchange gain of £16,250 deferred in the year to 30 September 2001 is then deemed to accrue in the year to 30 September 2002, so must be included in the calculations for that year.

(*c*)   Deferral relief is no longer available for accounting periods beginning on or after 1 October 2002, following the assimilation of the *FA 1993* rules on exchange gains and losses into those for loan relationships and derivative contracts. Transitional rules ensure that where a claim is made for deferral relief for the last accounting period subject to the *FA 1993* rules, the deferred amount will be brought into account under the new rules as a loan relationship credit. [*FA 2002, Sch 23 para 26*].

110   Groups of Companies

110.1 **SURPLUS SHADOW ACT: ALLOCATION AMONG GROUP MEMBERS** [*SI 1999 No 358*]

A Ltd owns 51% of the share capital of both B Ltd and C Ltd. The following information is relevant

Year ended 31.3.06	A Ltd £	B Ltd £	C Ltd £
(Loss)/Profits	(5,000)	40,000	55,000
Dividends paid (to companies other than to group companies)	40,000	35,000	8,000
Shadow ACT thereon	10,000	8,750	2,000
Year ended 31.3.07			
Profits	35,000	45,000	80,000
Dividends paid (other than to group companies)	30,000	40,000	40,000
Shadow ACT thereon	7,500	10,000	10,000

C Ltd has surplus ACT brought forward of £5,200 at 1 April 2005, not having been able to utilise it in prior years.

Year ended 31.3.06	£	A Ltd £	£	B Ltd £	£	C Ltd £
CT on profits at 19%		—		7,600		10,450
ACT capacity (note (*e*))		—	7,600		10,450	
Shadow ACT	10,000		8,750		2,000	
Surplus shadow ACT	10,000		1,150		—	
Spare ACT capacity		—		—	8,450	
Allocation by parent company (note (*a*))		(8,450)		—		(8,450)
Set-off of surplus ACT						—	—
Surplus shadow ACT c/fwd	1,550		1,150		—	
Surplus ACT c/fwd		—		—	5,200	
Mainstream corporation tax liability		—		7,600		10,450

Year ended 31.3.07	£	A Ltd £	£	B Ltd £	£	C Ltd £
CT on profits at 19%		6,650		8,550		15,200
ACT capacity	6,650		8,550		15,200	
Shadow ACT in year	7,500		10,000		10,000	
Shadow ACT b/fwd note (c)	1,550		1,150		—	
Surplus shadow ACT	2,400		2,600		—	
Spare ACT capacity	—		—		5,200	
Allocation by parent company	(2,400)		(2,600)		(5,000)	
Set-off of surplus ACT					200	(200)
Surplus ACT c/fwd	—		—		5,000	
Mainstream corporation tax liability		6,650		8,550		15,000

Notes

(a) Where a group company generates shadow ACT in excess of its capacity to utilise it, the parent company must allocate it to other group companies to the extent of their ACT capacity but not so as to displace their own shadow ACT. This is to ensure that no group member can get relief for surplus ACT brought forward until all group shadow ACT has been offset. Where total group shadow ACT exceeds total group capacity, the balance is to remain in the company in which the shadow ACT arose. In the year ended 31.3.06, A Ltd has chosen to allocate its own surplus shadow ACT to C Ltd before that of B Ltd.

(b) Where total group shadow ACT is less than the total group capacity, the parent company must determine which company is to receive the allocation of surplus shadow ACT. Thus, had there been a third subsidiary, D Ltd, with spare ACT capacity, A Ltd could have chosen to allocate the surplus shadow ACT to D Ltd to increase the capacity for set-off of surplus ACT in C Ltd.

(c) Any surplus shadow ACT carried forward is treated as shadow ACT paid in the following period.

(d) The Board of Inland Revenue may allocate the surplus shadow ACT where the parent company fails to do so but this can be overridden by a subsequent allocation by the parent company.

(e) Although the rate of ACT set-off is 20% (see 102.1, note (a) above), the set-off cannot be greater than the corporation tax payable.

(f) See 102.1 ADVANCE CORPORATION TAX for shadow ACT provisions generally.

110.2   Groups of Companies

110.2 **GROUP RELIEF** [*ICTA 1988, ss 402(1)(2), 403–403ZE, 413(3); FA 1998, s 38, Sch 5 para 29; FA 2002, s 84, Sch 30 para 2*]

(A)

A Ltd has a subsidiary company, B Ltd, in which it owns 75% of the ordinary share capital. Relevant information for the year ended 31 March 2007 is as follows

		£
A Ltd	Trading profit	30,000
	Property income	10,000
	Chargeable gain	15,000
	Charges paid	2,000
B Ltd	Trading loss	48,000
	Charges paid	2,000

In addition, B Ltd has trading losses brought forward of £25,000.

Group relief is available as follows

	£	£
A Ltd		
Trading profit		30,000
Property income		10,000
Chargeable gain		15,000
		55,000
Deduct Charges paid		2,000
Profits		53,000
Deduct Loss surrendered by B Ltd		50,000
Chargeable profits		£3,000
B Ltd		
Losses brought forward		25,000
Trading loss for the year	48,000	
Charges paid	2,000	
	50,000	
Deduct Loss surrendered to A Ltd	50,000	—
Losses carried forward		£25,000

(B)

A Ltd has two wholly owned subsidiaries B Ltd and C Ltd. There are no other associated companies. Results for the year ended 31 March 2007 are as follows

	£
A Ltd	
Trading profit	485,000
Chargeable gains	75,000
B Ltd	
Trading loss	92,000
Schedule D, Case III	6,000
Charges paid	4,000
C Ltd	
Trading profit	124,500
Schedule A	7,500

Disregarding group relief, the computation for each company is as follows

A Ltd

Total profits	£560,000
Corporation tax: (note (*a*))	
£560,000 at 30%	168,000

B Ltd

Total profits	6,000
Less: trading loss set against profits	6,000
Corporation tax liability	Nil
Trading loss unrelieved (£92,000 − £6,000)	86,000
Charges paid	4,000
Loss available for group relief	£90,000

C Ltd

Total profits	£132,000
Corporation tax: (note (*a*))	
£132,000 at 30%	39,600
Less: 11/400 × (£500,000 − £132,000) =	10,120
Corporation tax payable	£29,480

B Ltd surrenders its losses by group relief, £58,000 to A Ltd, £32,000 to C Ltd. The computations are then revised as follows

A Ltd

	£
Total profits	560,000
Less: group relief	58,000
Profits chargeable to corportion tax	£502,000
Corporation tax: (note (*a*))	
£502,000 at 30%	£150,600

B Ltd

Loss available for group relief	90,000
Less: losses surrendered	90,000

C Ltd

Total profits	132,000
Less: group relief	32,000
Profits chargeable to corporation tax	£100,000
Corporation tax: (note (*a*))	
£100,000 at 19%	£19,000

Notes

(*a*)   The upper and lower limits for profits to be chargeable at the small companies rate (£1,500,000 and £300,000) are divided by one plus the number of associated companies. They are thus £500,000 and £100,000 in this case.

110.3 Groups of Companies

(b) The surrenders as above achieve the maximum tax saving. Any switch of relief from A Ltd to C Ltd saves tax in C Ltd at 19% but at the cost of extra tax in A Ltd at 30%. Any switch from C Ltd to A Ltd saves tax in A Ltd at 30% but at the cost of extra tax in C Ltd at the effective marginal rate of 32.75%.

110.3 **KINDS OF GROUP RELIEF** [*ICTA 1988, ss 393(9), 403–403ZE; FA 1998, s 38(1), Sch 5 para 29; FA 2002, s 84, Sch 30 para 2*]

A Ltd is an investment company which has three trading subsidiaries, B Ltd, C Ltd and D Ltd in which it owns 100% of the share capital. The companies have the following results for the two years ending 31 March 2007.

		Year ended 31.3.06 £	Year ended 31.3.07 £
A Ltd	Profits	10,000	20,000
	Management expenses	(20,000)	(50,000)
B Ltd	Trading loss	(10,000)	(10,000)
	Schedule A income (after capital allowances)		30,000
	Non-trading loan relationship deficit		(10,000)
C Ltd	Trading profit/(loss)	(10,000)	30,000
	Schedule A income		1,000
	Capital allowances — trading assets		(5,000)
	— Schedule A assets		(2,000)
	Management expenses		(40,000)
D Ltd	Profits		70,000

Group relief may be claimed for trading losses, management expenses, Schedule A losses and charges on income, as follows

		Year ended 31.3.06 £	Year ended 31.3.07 £
A Ltd			
Profits		10,000	20,000
Management expenses		(20,000)	(50,000)
Excess management expenses		(10,000)	(30,000)
Deduct Surrendered to D Ltd		—	30,000
Management expenses carried forward to year ended 31.3.08	(note (*a*))	£(10,000)	—
B Ltd			
Trading loss brought forward		—	(10,000)
Trading loss		(10,000)	(10,000)
Trading loss carried forward		£(10,000)	—
			(20,000)
Deduct Surrendered to D Ltd	(note (*b*))		10,000
Trading loss carried forward (not available for group relief or set-off against non-trading income)			£(10,000)
Non-trading loan relationship deficit	(note (*b*))		(10,000)
Deduct Surrendered to D Ltd			10,000
Profits chargeable to corporation tax			£30,000
C Ltd			
Trading loss brought forward		—	(10,000)
Trading loss		(10,000)	
Trading loss carried forward		£(10,000)	
Trading profit (£30,000) *less* trade capital allowances (£5,000)			25,000
			15,000
Schedule A income (£1,000) less Schedule A capital allowances (£2,000) less surrendered to D Ltd (£1,000)	(note (*c*))		–
			15,000
Management expenses (£40,000) less surrendered to D Ltd (£15,000)	(note (*c*))		(25,000)
Management expenses carried forward			£(10,000)

110.3 Groups of Companies

D Ltd — year ended 31.3.07	£	£
Profits		70,000
Deduct Surrendered by A Ltd	30,000	
Surrendered by B Ltd		
trading loss	10,000	
loan relationship deficit	10,000	
Surrendered by C Ltd		
Schedule A losses and management expenses	16,000	66,000
Profits chargeable to corporation tax		£4,000

Notes

(a) It is not possible in the year ended 31 March 2007 to deduct the excess management expenses brought forward from the year ended 31 March 2006 before deducting the current year management expenses to arrive at the amount available for group relief. The excess management expenses of £10,000 arising in the year ended 31 March 2006 are carried forward to the year ended 31 March 2007 but may not be surrendered and are, therefore, treated as carried forward from the year ended 31 March 2007. [*ICTA 1988, s 403ZD(4)*]. See also note (d).

(b) Although a company might normally relieve a trading loss and a non-trading loan relationship deficit against other income of the year before surrendering the loss or deficit, it is not obliged to do so. Thus, B Ltd could have reduced its chargeable profits in the year ended 31 March 2006 by £20,000 instead of surrendering that amount to D Ltd. [*ICTA 1988, ss 403ZA, 403ZC*].

(c) Charges on income, Schedule A losses, management expenses and non-trading losses on intangible assets can be surrendered as group relief only to the extent that in aggregate they exceed the surrendering company's 'gross profits' for the accounting period. The 'gross profits' of the accounting period are, broadly, the profits of the period without any deduction for any amounts qualifying for group relief relating to that period or any amounts of any other period. [*ICTA 1988, ss 403(3), 403ZD; FA 1998, Sch 5 para 29; FA 2002, Sch 30 para 2*]. Therefore, the amount which C Ltd can surrender as group relief is restricted as follows

Management expenses	40,000
Schedule A loss	1,000
	41,000
Deduct gross profits (before *ICTA 1988, s 393(1)* relief)	25,000
Group relief	£16,000 .

The amount surrendered is taken to consist first of charges, then of Schedule A losses, then of management expenses, and finally of losses on intangible assets. The amount surrendered by C Ltd is therefore identified as the Schedule A loss of £1,000 and management expenses of £15,000.

C Ltd's management expenses have been relieved as follows

Management expenses	40,000
Deduct Management expenses relieved against income	(15,000)
Surrendered to D Ltd	(15,000)
Excess management expenses carried forward	£10,000

110.4 GROUP RELIEF 'OVERLAPPING PERIODS'

[*ICTA 1988, ss 403–403B; F(No 2)A 1997, s 41, Sch 7 paras 2,3,9*]
D Ltd has several wholly owned subsidiaries, including E Ltd and F Ltd. D Ltd prepares accounts to 30 September, the other two companies to 31 December. Their results were as follows

			£
D Ltd	year ended 30.9.06	loss	(240,000)
E Ltd	year ended 31.12.06	profit	120,000
F Ltd	year ended 31.12.06	profit	150,000

D Ltd makes a profit for the year ended 30.9.07.

The overlapping period is the nine months to 30.9.06. The surrenderable amount of D Ltd's loss for the overlapping period is $\frac{9}{12}$ x £240,000 = £180,000. D Ltd surrenders the loss as follows

(i)   Surrender to E Ltd — see note (*a*)

		£
Surrender the smaller of:		
Unused part of the surrenderable amount for		
the overlapping period		180,000
Unrelieved part of E Ltd's total profits for the		
overlapping period	$\frac{9}{12} \times$ £120,000	90,000
Surrender		£90,000

(ii)   Surrender to F Ltd — see note (*b*)

		£	£
Surrender the smaller of:			
Unused part of the surrenderable amount			
for the overlapping period			
surrenderable amount		180,000	
deduct amount surrendered to E Ltd		90,000	90,000
Unrelieved part of F Ltd's total profits for			
the overlapping period	$\frac{9}{12} \times$ £150,000		112,500
Surrender			£90,000

Notes

(*a*)   The effect of the rules is to restrict the overall surrender by D Ltd to $\frac{9}{12}$ of its loss for the year ended 30 September 2006.

(*b*)   Where more than one claim relates to the whole or part of the same overlapping period, the claims must be considered in the order in which they are made (determined by the date on which the claim ceases to be capable of being withdrawn). Where, as in this case, two or more claims are deemed to be made at the same time, they are treated as made in such order as the companies involved may elect. In the absence of such an election, an officer of the Board may direct. [*ICTA 1998, s 403A(6)(7); F(No 2)A 1997, s 41, Sch 7 paras 2, 9*].

110.5 Groups of Companies

110.5 GROUP RELIEF: COMPANIES JOINING OR LEAVING THE GROUP [*ICTA 1988, ss 402–403B; F(No 2)A 1997, s 41, Sch 7 paras 2, 9*]
On 1 April 2006 B Ltd was held as to 90% by A Ltd and 10% by a non-resident.
On 1 September 2006 C Ltd became a 75% subsidiary of A Ltd.
On 31 December 2006 A Ltd sells 30% of the shares in B Ltd (retaining 60%). A Ltd, B Ltd and C Ltd all prepare accounts to 31 March each year. During the year ended 31 March 2007 the results of the companies are as follows

A Ltd	Profit	£60,000
B Ltd	Loss	£(240,000)
C Ltd	Profit	£30,000

Group relief for the loss sustained by B Ltd in the year ended 31.3.07 is available as follows

Overlapping periods

Loss making period   1.4.06   30.6.06   1.9.06   31.12.06   31.3.07

Period for which B Ltd was a
'75% subsidiary' of A Ltd   ├──────── 9 months ────────┤

Period for which B Ltd and C Ltd
were '75% subsidiaries' of A Ltd   ├─4 months ─┤

Calculation of loss relieved

(i) Against profits of A Ltd
Smaller of:

Unused part of the surrenderable amount for the overlapping period	$\frac{9}{12} \times £240,000$	£180,000
Unrelieved part of A Ltd's total profits for the overlapping period	$\frac{9}{12} \times £60,000$	£45,000
Therefore, loss relieved		£45,000

(ii) Against profits of C Ltd

		£	£
Smaller of:			
Unused part of the surrenderable amount for the overlapping period			
surrenderable amount	$\frac{4}{12} \times £240,000$	80,000	
deduct proportion of amount surrendered to A Ltd relating to overlapping period	$\frac{4}{9} \times £45,000$	20,000	60,000
Unrelieved part of C Ltd's total profits for the overlapping period	$\frac{4}{12} \times £30,000$		10,000
Therefore, loss relieved			£10,000

Summary

	A Ltd	B Ltd	C Ltd
	£	£	£
Profit/(loss)	60,000	(240,000)	30,000
Group relief (claim)/surrender	(45,000)	55,000	(10,000)
Chargeable profit/(loss carried forward)	£15,000	£(185,000)	£20,000

Notes

(a) When a company joins or leaves a group, the profit or loss is apportioned on a time basis unless this method would work unreasonably or unjustly. In the latter event a just and reasonable method of apportionment shall be used. [*ICTA 1988, s 403B*].

(b) See notes (a) and (b) to 110.4 above.

110.6 **GROUP RELIEF: RELATIONSHIP TO OTHER RELIEFS** [*ICTA 1988, ss 338(1), 393(1)(9), 393A, 402, 403, 407; FA 1991, s 73, Sch 15 paras 13, 14; FA 1998, Sch 5 para 29*]

B Ltd is a subsidiary of A Ltd and commenced trading on 1 April 2003. Both companies prepare accounts to 31 March each year. The results for the three years ended 31 March 2007 were as follows.

				£
A Ltd	year ended 31 March	2005	Loss	(4,000)
		2006	Loss	(3,000)
		2007	Loss	(5,000)
B Ltd	year ended 31 March	2005	Loss	(5,000)
		2006	Profit	10,000
		2007	Loss	(20,000)
		2005	Schedule A income	1,000
		2006	Schedule A income	1,000
		2007	Schedule A income	1,000
		2005	Non-trade charges paid	(1,000)
		2006	Non-trade charges paid	(1,000)
		2007	Non-trade charges paid	(1,000)
		2007	Chargeable gains	5,000

110.6   Groups of Companies

The losses can be used as follows

	Year ended 31.3.05 £	Year ended 31.3.06 £	Year ended 31.3.07 £
B Ltd			
Trading profit/(loss)	(5,000)	10,000	(20,000)
Schedule D, Case I	—	10,000	—
ICTA 1988, s 393(1) loss relief	—	(4,000)	—
Schedule A	1,000	1,000	1,000
Income	1,000	7,000	1,000
Chargeable gains	—	—	5,000
ICTA 1988, s 393A(1)(a) loss relief	(1,000)	—	(6,000)
Profits subject to group relief	—	7,000	—
Losses surrendered by A Ltd	—	(3,000)	—
	—	4,000	—
ICTA 1988, s 393A(1)(b) loss relief	—	(4,000)	—
Chargeable profits	—	—	—
Losses brought forward	—	(4,000)	—
Loss of the period	(5,000)	—	(20,000)
ICTA 1988, s 393(1) relief	—	4,000	—
ICTA 1988, s 393A(1)(a) relief	1,000	—	6,000
ICTA 1988, s 393A(1)(b) relief	—	—	4,000
Losses carried forward	£(4,000)	—	£(10,000)
Unrelieved non-trade charges	£(1,000)	£(1,000)	£(1,000)
A Ltd			
Trading loss	4,000	3,000	5,000
Deduct Surrendered to B Ltd	—	(3,000)	—
	4,000	—	5,000
Loss brought forward	—	4,000	4,000
Loss (not available for group relief) carried forward	£4,000	£4,000	£9,000

Notes

(a)   Losses brought forward from previous periods must be used before claiming group relief, as must losses incurred in the current period and available for set-off under *ICTA 1988, s 393A(1)(a)*. However, group relief takes priority to losses carried back from subsequent periods under *ICTA 1988, s 393A(1)(b)*.

(b)   Relief for losses carried back under *ICTA 1988, s 393A(1)(b)* is given after trade charges but before non-trade charges. Non-trade charges cannot be carried forward and excess charges, whether trade or non-trade, cannot be carried back. See also 118.3(A) LOSSES.

110.7 **CONSORTIUM RELIEF**

(A) Loss by company owned by consortium [*ICTA 1988, ss 402(3)(a), 403–403C; F(No2)A 1997, s 41, Sch 7 paras 2, 9; FA 1998, s 81*]

On 1 April 2006 the share capital of E Ltd was owned as follows

	%
A Ltd	40
B Ltd	40
C Ltd	20
	100

All the companies were UK resident for tax purposes.

During the year ended 31 March 2007 the following events took place

| On 1.7.06 | D Ltd bought | 20% from A Ltd |
| On 1.10.06 | C Ltd bought | 10% from B Ltd |

The companies had the following results for the year ended 31 March 2007

		£
A Ltd	Profit	40,000
B Ltd	Profit	33,000
C Ltd	Profit	10,000
D Ltd	Profit	18,000
E Ltd	Loss	(100,000)

All the member companies claim consortium relief in respect of the loss sustained by E Ltd. The companies elect that the claims be treated as made first by A Ltd, then by B Ltd, C Ltd and finally by D Ltd. For each company the consortium relief available is the lowest of the following three amounts:

(i)   the unused part of the surrenderable amount for the overlapping period;
(ii) the unrelieved part of the claimant company's total profits for the overlapping period; and
(iii) the surrenderable amount for the overlapping period multiplied by the claimant member's share in the consortium in that period.

[*F(No 2)A 1997, s 41, Sch 7 paras 2, 9; FA 1998, s 81*]

A Ltd

The overlapping period is the twelve months to 31.3.07. The amounts are

		£
(i)		100,000
(ii)		40,000
(iii)	$100,000 \times 25\%$ $(40\% \times \frac{3}{12} + 20\% \times \frac{9}{12})$	25,000

Therefore, loss relieved £25,000

73

110.7 Groups of Companies

B Ltd
The overlapping period is the twelve months to 31.3.07. The amounts are

		£	£
(i)	Surrenderable amount	100,000	
	Deduct loss previously surrendered	25,000	75,000
(ii)			33,000
(iii)	$100,000 \times 35\% \ (40\% \times \frac{6}{12} + 30\% \times \frac{6}{12})$		35,000
Therefore, loss relieved			£33,000

C Ltd
The overlapping period is the twelve months to 31.3.07. The amounts are

		£	£
(i)	Surrenderable amount	100,000	
	Deduct losses previously surrendered (£25,000 + £33,000)	58,000	42,000
(ii)			10,000
(iii)	$100,000 \times 25\% \ (20\% \times \frac{6}{12} + 30\% \times \frac{6}{12})$		25,000
Therefore, loss relieved			£10,000

D Ltd
As D Ltd only became a member of the consortium on 1.7.06, the overlapping period is the nine months to 31.3.07. The amounts are

		£	£
(i)	Surrenderable amount $100,000 \times \frac{9}{12}$	75,000	
	Deduct $\frac{9}{12} \times$ losses previously surrendered (£25,000 + £33,000 + £10,000)	51,000	24,000
(ii)	$18,000 \times \frac{9}{12}$		13,500
(iii)	$100,000 \times \frac{9}{12} \times 20\%$		15,000
Therefore, loss relieved			£13,500

Summary

	A Ltd £	B Ltd £	C Ltd £	D Ltd £
Profits for the year ended 31.3.07	40,000	33,000	10,000	18,000
Deduct Loss surrendered by E Ltd	(25,000)	(33,000)	(10,000)	(13,500)
Chargeable profits	£15,000	—	—	£4,500

E Ltd

		£	Losses £
Loss for the year ended 31.3.07			100,000
Deduct Loss surrendered to	A Ltd	(25,000)	
	B Ltd	(33,000)	
	C Ltd	(10,000)	
	D Ltd	(13,500)	(81,500)
Not available for consortium relief			£18,500

(B) Loss by company owned by consortium: claim by member of consortium company's group [*ICTA 1988, ss 405(1)–(3), 406(1)–(4), 413(2)*]

A Ltd owns 100% of the share capital of B Ltd
B Ltd owns 40% of the share capital of D Ltd
C Ltd owns 60% of the share capital of D Ltd
D Ltd owns 100% of the share capital of E Ltd
D Ltd owns 100% of the share capital of F Ltd

This can be shown as follows

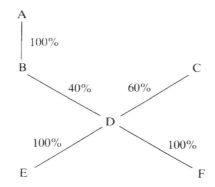

There are two groups, A and B, and D, E and F. D is owned by a consortium of B and C. This relationship has existed for a number of years with all companies having the same accounting periods. None of the companies has any losses brought forward.

The companies have the following results for year ended 31 July 2006

A Ltd   £100,000 profit
B Ltd   £(30,000) loss
C Ltd   £Nil
D Ltd   £(20,000) loss
E Ltd   £10,000 profit
F Ltd   £(3,000) loss

110.7 Groups of Companies

E Ltd claims group relief as follows

		£	£
Profit			10,000
Deduct Group relief: loss surrendered by F Ltd (note (*b*))	3,000	
Group relief: loss surrendered by D Ltd (note (*b*))	7,000	(10,000)
		—

A Ltd can claim group relief and consortium relief as follows

		£	£
Profit			100,000
Deduct Group relief: loss surrendered by B Ltd (note (*c*))	30,000	
Consortium relief: loss surrendered by D Ltd (note (*d*))	5,200	(35,200)
Chargeable profit			£64,800

Notes

(*a*) Where a company owned by a consortium is also a member of a group, its losses may be surrendered partly as group relief and partly as consortium relief.

(*b*) Where a loss of a company owned by a consortium or of a company within its group may be used both as group relief and consortium relief, the consortium relief is restricted. In determining the amount of consortium relief available, it is assumed that the maximum possible group relief is deducted after taking account of any other actual group relief claims within the consortium owned company's group. [*ICTA 1988, s 405(1)–(3)*]. As F Ltd has surrendered losses of £3,000 to E Ltd, D Ltd can only surrender £7,000 to E Ltd as group relief. The surrenderable amount for the period for the purpose of consortium relief is restricted to the balance of D Ltd's loss, i.e. £13,000. If E Ltd had not claimed £3,000 group relief for F Ltd's loss, D Ltd could have surrendered £10,000 to E Ltd by way of group relief and this would have reduced D Ltd's surrenderable amount for consortium relief purposes to £10,000.

(*c*) Group relief available to A Ltd is the lower of £100,000 and £30,000.

(*d*) Consortium relief available to A Ltd is the lower of £13,000 (the unused surrenderable amount for the period), £70,000 (its unrelieved profits for the period (£100,000 less £30,000 group relief previously claimed) and £5,200 (40% of £13,000). The relief available to A Ltd is the same as that which B Ltd could have claimed if it had had sufficient profits. A Ltd could also have claimed consortium relief in respect of F Ltd's loss if that had exceeded the £10,000 necessary to cover E Ltd's profit. [*ICTA 1988, s 406(1)–(4)*].

(C) Loss by subsidiary of company owned by consortium [*ICTA 1988, ss 402(3)(b), 403(1), 403C, 413(7)–(10)*]
Throughout 2006 the share capital of E Ltd was owned as follows

	%
A Ltd	35
B Ltd	30
C Ltd	25
D Ltd	10
	100

E Ltd owned 90% of the share capital of F Ltd, a trading company. The companies had the following results for the year ended 31 December 2006.

		£
A Ltd	Profit	100,000
B Ltd	Loss	(40,000)
C Ltd	Profit	30,000
D Ltd	Profit	80,000
E Ltd	Profit	40,000
F Ltd	Loss	(240,000)

All the above companies were UK resident for tax purposes.

Group relief of £40,000 of the loss sustained by F Ltd is claimed by E Ltd (note (c)).

Consortium relief for the loss sustained by F Ltd would be available as follows

	A Ltd £	B Ltd £	C Ltd £	D Ltd £
Profits for the year ended 31.12.06	100,000	—	30,000	80,000
Deduct Loss surrendered by				
F Ltd (note (a))	(70,000)	—	(30,000)	(20,000)
Chargeable profits	£30,000	—	—	£60,000

		£	Losses £
F Ltd			
Loss for the year ended 31.12.06			240,000
Deduct Loss surrendered to E Ltd			(40,000)
Available for consortium relief			200,000
Deduct Loss surrendered to	A Ltd	(70,000)	
	C Ltd	(30,000)	
	D Ltd	(20,000)	(120,000)
Losses carried forward			£80,000

Notes

(a)   Loss relief for each consortium member is the lower of

   (i)   the unused part of the surrenderable amount for the year;

   (ii)   the unrelieved part of the claimant company's total profits for the year; and

   (iii) the surrenderable amount for the year multiplied by the claimant member's share in the consortium.

In this instance, the order in which the claims are deemed to be made does not affect the amounts which can be claimed, as (i) is greater than (ii) and (iii) in all cases.

(*b*)   The surrenderable amount (see note (*c*)) multiplied by the share in the consortium appropriate to each member is

	%	£
A Ltd	35	70,000
B Ltd	30	60,000
C Ltd	25	50,000
D Ltd	10	20,000
	100	£200,000

(*c*)   The loss available for consortium relief (the surrenderable amount) is reduced by any potentially available group relief. See also notes (*a*) and (*b*) to (B) above.

(D) Loss by consortium member [*ICTA 1988, ss 402(3), 403A–C*]
A Ltd, B Ltd, C Ltd and D Ltd have for many years held 40%, 30%, 20% and 10% respectively of the ordinary share capital of E Ltd. All five companies are UK resident and have always previously had taxable profits. However, for the year ending 30 June 2006 D Ltd has a tax loss of £100,000, followed by taxable profits of £40,000 for the subsequent year. E Ltd's taxable profits are £80,000 and £140,000 for the two years ending 31 December 2004 and 31 December 2005 respectively.

With the consent of A Ltd, B Ltd and C Ltd, D Ltd can (if it wishes) surrender the following part of its loss of £100,000 to E Ltd (assuming no other group/consortium relief claims are made involving either company)

Overlapping period 1.7.05 to 31.12.05
Unused part of the surrenderable amount for
the overlapping period $\frac{6}{12}$ × £100,000 £50,000
Unrelieved part of E Ltd's total profits for the
overlapping period $\frac{6}{12}$ × £80,000 £40,000
E Ltd's total profits for the overlapping period
multiplied by D Ltd's share in consortium $\frac{6}{12}$ × £80,000 × 10% £4,000

Overlapping period 1.1.06 to 30.6.06
Unused part of the surrenderable amount for
the overlapping period $\frac{6}{12}$ × £100,000 £50,000
Unrelieved part of E Ltd's total profits for the
overlapping period $\frac{6}{12}$ × £140,000 £70,000
E Ltd's total profits for the overlapping period
multiplied by D Ltd's share in consortium $\frac{6}{12}$ × £140,000 × 10% £7,000

The lowest figures for the two periods are £4,000 and £7,000.

Therefore, E Ltd can claim £4,000 of D Ltd's loss against its own profits for the year ended 31.12.05 and £7,000 against its profits for the year ending 31.12.06.

111   Income Tax in relation to a Company

111.1 **ACCOUNTING FOR INCOME TAX ON RECEIPTS AND PAYMENTS** [*ICTA 1988, ss 7(2), 349–349D, Sch 16; FA 1990, s 98(2), Sch 19 Pt V; FA 2001, s 85*]

S Ltd, a company with two associated companies, prepares accounts each year to 31 October. During the two years ending 31 October 2006 it pays and receives several sums (not being interest) from which basic rate income tax is deducted.

The following items are shown net

	Receipts £	Payments £
21.12.04		7,800
4.1.05	3,900	
9.8.05	7,800	
24.10.05	11,700	
25.3.06		7,800
14.8.06		9,360

The adjusted profits (*before* taking account of the gross equivalents of the above amounts) were

	£
Year ended 31.10.05	630,000
Year ended 31.10.06	860,000

S Ltd will use the following figures in connection with the CT61 returns rendered to HMRC and will also be able to set off against its corporation tax liability the income tax suffered as shown

Return period	Payments £	Receipts £	Cumulative payments less receipts £	Income tax paid/ (repaid) with return £
Year ended 31.10.05				
1.11.04 to 31.12.04	7,800		7,800	2,200
1.1.05 to 31.3.05		3,900	3,900	(1,100)
1.4.05 to 30.6.05 (No return)			3,900	
1.7.05 to 30.9.05		7,800	(3,900)	(1,100)
1.10.05 to 31.10.05		11,700	(15,600)	
				—
Year ended 31.10.06				
1.11.05 to 31.12.05 (No return)				
1.1.06 to 31.3.06	7,800		7,800	2,200
1.4.06 to 30.6.06 (No return)			7,800	
1.7.06 to 30.9.06 (No return)	9,360		17,160	2,640
1.10.06 to 31.10.06 (No return)			17,160	
				£4,840

111.1   Income Tax in relation to a Company

Taxable profits

	Year ended 31.10.05 £	Year ended 31.10.06 £
Adjusted profits as stated	630,000	860,000
Add Cumulative receipts £15,600 + tax £4,400	20,000	
Deduct Cumulative payments £17,160 + tax of £4,840		22,000
Taxable profits	£650,000	£838,000

Tax payable

		Year ended 31.10.05 £	Year ended 31.10.06 £
CT @ 30% on profits		195,000	251,400
Deduct Income tax suffered	(note (*a*))	4,400	
Net liability		£190,600	£251,400

Notes

(*a*)   This represents tax suffered on receipts, less that which has been offset against tax deducted from payments.

	£
Tax on receipts	6,600
Tax deducted from payments and recovered from HMRC	2,200
	£4,400

(*b*)   Payments made by companies after 31 March 2001 under the following provisions do not have to be made under deduction of income tax where the company reasonably believes that, at the time of payment, the recipient is either a UK company (or a partnership of such companies) or a non-UK resident company trading in the UK through a branch or agency and in computing whose profits the payment falls to be brought into account. The provisions concerned are:

　　(i)　*ICTA 1988, s 349(1)* (annuities and other annual payments and royalties and other sums paid for the use of UK patents);

　　(ii)　*ICTA 1988, s 349(2)(a)(b)* (UK interest);

　　(iii)　*ICTA 1988, s 349(3A)* (dividends or interest on securities issued by building societies); and

　　(iv)　*ICTA 1988, s 524(3)(b)* (proceeds of sale of UK patent rights).

(*c*)   Payments made by companies or local authorities after 30 September 2002 do not have to be made under deduction of income tax where the company or local authority reasonably believe that, at the time of the payment, either the conditions in (*b*) above are satisfied, or the payment is made to certain bodies or persons as specified in *ICTA 1988, s 349B(3)–(7)*.

[*ICTA 1988, ss 349A–349D; FA 2001, s 85; FA 2002, s 94*].

112   Intangible Assets

112.1 **DEBITS AND CREDITS** [*FA 2002, Sch 29 paras 7–29*]

(A) Writing-down on accounting basis

On 1 April 2003, Oval Ltd purchased an intangible asset from an unrelated company, Edgbaston Ltd, for £100,000. The asset is to be used for trading purposes and has a remaining useful economic life of 15 years. The cost of the asset is capitalised in Oval Ltd's accounts and in accordance with generally accepted accounting practice is amortised on a straight-line basis over the remaining 15 year life. On 1 April 2006, the company sells the asset to another unrelated company, Riverside Ltd, for £150,000.

Oval Ltd will bring into account for tax purposes the following debits and credits in respect of the intangible asset.

	£
Y/e 31.3.04	
Cost of asset	100,000
Debit for year (1/15 of cost)	(6,667)
WDV at 31.3.04	93,333
Y/e 31.3.05	
Debit for year (1/15 of cost)	(6,667)
WDV at 31.3.05	86,666
Y/e 31.3.06	
Debit for year (1/15 of cost)	(6,667)
WDV at 31.3.06	£80,000
Y/e 31.3.07	
Proceeds of realisation	150,000
Less Tax written-down value	80,000
Taxable credit	£70,000

As the asset was held for trading purposes, the debits of £6,667 for each of the years ended 31 March 2004, 2005 and 2006 are allowable trading deductions, and the credit of £70,000 for the year ended 31 March 2007 is a trading receipt.

Note

(*a*) See 112.3 below for the rollover relief available on reinvestment of disposal proceeds in new intangible assets.

(B) Writing-down at fixed rate

On 1 January 2004, M Ltd, which draws up accounts each year to 31 December, purchases the trade of X Ltd, an unrelated company. It is agreed that, of the purchase price, £500,000 is allocated to X Ltd's brand name, which is particularly well established in the UK and the USA. The brand name is considered to have an indefinite economic life and accordingly the expenditure is not amortised in M Ltd's accounts. Before 31 December 2006 M Ltd elects to write down the cost at the fixed rate of 4% per year. On 1 January 2006, M Ltd sells its rights to the brand name in the USA for £400,000 to Z plc, an unrelated company. £250,000 of the book value of the brand name in the accounts is set off against the disposal, giving an accounting profit of £150,000, and leaving the remaining book value as £250,000. On 1 January 2008, M Ltd sells the remaining rights in the brand name to Z plc for £200,000.

112.1   Intangible Assets

M Ltd must bring into account in calculating its trading profits the following debits and credits in respect of the brand name.

	£
Y/e 31.12.04	
Cost of brand name	500,000
Debit for year (4% of cost)	(20,000)
WDV at 31.12.04	480,000
Y/e 31.12.05	
Debit for year (4% of cost)	(20,000)
WDV at 31.12.05	£460,000
Y/e 31.12.06	
Part-realisation proceeds	400,000
Less Adjusted WDV (note (*b*))	230,000
Gain on part realisation (credit)	£170,000
Adjusted WDV of asset after part realisation (note (*c*))	230,000
Debit for year (4% of cost of remaining asset (note (*d*))	(10,000)
WDV at 31.12.06	220,000
Y/e 31.12.07	
Debit for year (4% of remaining cost)	(10,000)
WDV at 31.12.07	£210,000
Y/e 31.12.08	
Realisation proceeds	200,000
Less WDV at 31.12.07	210,000
Loss on realisation (debit)	£(10,000)

Notes

(*a*)   A company may elect for the tax cost of an intangible asset to be written down for tax purposes at a fixed rate. The election must be made in writing to HMRC within two years after the end of the accounting period in which the asset is created or acquired by the company and is irrevocable. Where the election is made, a debit of 4% of the cost (or, if less, the balance of the written-down value) is brought into account in each accounting period beginning with that in which the expenditure is incurred. The debit is proportionately reduced for accounting periods of less than twelve months. [*FA 2002, Sch 29 paras 10, 11*].

(*b*)   On the part realisation of an asset, a proportion of the written-down value of the asset is deducted from the proceeds to arrive at the amount of the credit or debit arising. The proportion is that given by dividing the reduction in accounting value (i.e. the accounting value immediatley before the realisation less the accounting value immediately afterwards) by the accounting value immediately before the realisation. [*FA 2002, Sch 29 para 22*]. In this case, the reduction in accounting value is (£500,000 – £250,000) = £250,000, and the accounting value immediately before the realisation is £500,000. The amount to be deducted from the proceeds in this case is therefore £460,000 × (£250,000/£500,000) = £230,000.

(c) Following a part realisation, the written-down value of the remaining part of the asset is reduced to that proportion of it that is equal to the accounting value immediately after the realisation divided by the accounting value immediately before the realisation. [FA 2002, Sch 29 para 29(1)(2)]. In this case, therefore, the adjusted written-down value is £460,000 × (£250,000/£500,000) = £230,000.

(d) Following a part realisation, the fixed rate debit is calculated by reference to 4% of the value of the asset recognised for accounting purposes immediately after the realisation (plus the cost of any subsequent capitalised expenditure on the asset). [FA 2002, Sch 29 para 11(5)].

112.2 **NON-TRADING LOSS ON INTANGIBLE ASSETS** [FA 2002, Sch 29 paras 34, 35]
A Ltd is an investment company drawing up accounts each year to 31 March. The following figures are relevant for the two years ended 31 March 2006 and 2007.

	Y/e 31.3.06 £	Y/e 31.3.07 £
Schedule A profits	15,000	16,000
Schedule D, Case III	5,000	20,000
Schedule D, Case V (foreign tax paid £2,375)	20,000	—
Management expenses	5,000	5,000
Non–trading profit/(loss) on intangible fixed assets	(55,000)	11,000

A Ltd wishes to make the most tax-efficient use of the non-trading loss, and so makes a claim to set off £15,000 against profits of the year ended 31 March 2006 under FA 2002, Sch 29 para 35(1). The corporation tax computations for the two years ended 31 March 2007 are as follows.

	£
Y/e 31.3.06	
Schedule A	15,000
Schedule D, Case III	5,000
Schedule D, Case V	20,000
	40,000
Deduct Management expenses	5,000
Non-trading loss	15,000
Profits chargeable to CT	£20,000
Corporation tax: £20,000 @ 0%/23.75%	2,375
Deduct Double tax relief	2,375
Corporation tax payable	Nil

112.2   Intangible Assets

	£
Y/e 31.3.07	
Schedule A	16,000
Schedule D, Case III	20,000
Schedule D, Case VI (see below)	—
	36,000
Deduct Management expenses	5,000
Non-trading loss	29,000
Profits chargeable to CT	£2,000
Corporation tax: £2,000 @ 19%	£380

Use of non–trading loss

	£
Loss y/e 31.3.06	55,000
Set-off against profits for y/e 31.3.06	15,000
Carry-forward as non–trading debit	£40,000
Y/e 31.3.07	
Non-trading profit of period	11,000
Deduct Non-trading debit brought forward	40,000
Non-trading loss set off against profits for y/e 31.3.07	£29,000

Notes

(a) A non-trading loss on intangible fixed assets for an accounting period may be set off against the company's total profits for the period. The company must make a claim for relief within two years after the end of the accounting period, or within such further period as HMRC may allow. Relief for the whole or part of the loss may be claimed in this way. [*FA 2002, Sch 29 para 35(1)(2)*].

(b) A non-trading loss may alternatively be surrendered as group relief. See 110.3 GROUPS OF COMPANIES.

(c) To the extent that a non-trading loss is not set off against profits of the current accounting period or surrendered as group relief, it is carried forward to the next accounting period and treated as a non-trading debit of that period. [*FA 2002, Sch 29 para 35(3)*]. The carried-forward loss is therefore included in the computation of any profit or loss on intangible fixed assets for that period. Where a loss results, the whole loss is available for set-off against total profits of the period. However, the debit carried forward must be excluded from the loss for the period in calculating any amount available for surrender as group relief. [*ICTA 1988, s 403ZD(6); FA 2002, s 84(2), Sch 30 para 2(2)*].

112.3 **ROLLOVER RELIEF ON REINVESTMENT** [*FA 2002, Sch 29 paras 37–45*]
Oval Ltd, the company in 112.1(A) above, purchases a new intangible fixed asset (asset 2) on 1 April 2008 for £165,000 and claims rollover relief in respect of the asset disposed of in that example (referred to below as asset 1).

The effect of the claim for tax purposes is as follows.

	£
Disposal proceeds of asset 1	150,000
Tax cost of asset 1	100,000
Rollover relief available	£50,000

The taxable credit on disposal of asset 1 for the year ended 31.3.07 is therefore recalculated as follows

	£
Proceeds of realisation	150,000
Less Tax written-down value	80,000
Amount rolled over	50,000
Taxable credit	£20,000

The cost for tax purposes of asset 2 is adjusted as follows

	£
Cost of asset 2	165,000
Less amount rolled over on asset 1	50,000
Adjusted cost for tax purposes	£115,000

Notes

(*a*)   A company which realises a chargeable intangible asset and incurs expenditure on other chargeable intangible assets within the period beginning one year before the date of realisation and ending three years after that date, may, subject to meeting detailed conditions, claim rollover relief under *FA 2002, Sch 29 Pt 7*. The claim must specify the old assets to which the claim relates, the expenditure on other assets by reference to which relief is claimed, and the amount of relief claimed. [*FA 2002, Sch 29 para 40*].

(*b*)   On making the claim, the proceeds of realisation of the old asset and the cost recognised for tax purposes of the other assets are both reduced by the amount available for relief. Where the expenditure on the other assets is equal to or exceeds the realisation proceeds the amount available for relief is the excess of the proceeds over the tax cost of the original asset. Where the expenditure on other assets is less than the realisation proceeds, the amount available for relief is the excess of the expenditure over the tax cost of the original asset. The relief does not affect the tax treatment of the other parties to the transactions. [*FA 2002, Sch 29 para 41*].

(*c*)   In this case, the relief available is £50,000, leaving £20,000 of the gain on realisation chargeable. This effectively recovers the debits previously given in respect of the asset (£6,667 × 3 = £20,000, see 112.1(A) above). Only the profit element is rolled over.

113   Interest on Overpaid Tax

[ICTA 1988, ss 825, 826; FA 1989, s 178; FA 1991, Sch 15 para 22, 23; SI 1989 No 1297; SI 1993 No 2212]

113.1 **(A) Repayment of tax: general** *[SI 1998 No 3175 and SI 1998 No 3176]*

X Ltd prepares accounts to 31 December. On 15 June 2006 it submits its tax return for the year ended 31 December 2005 showing a corporation tax liability for the period of £14,000, and accompanied by a payment of £7,000. On 1 October 2006 it makes a further payment of £7,000. It subsequently submits an amended return showing a reduced liability of £12,500, and £1,500 is repaid to the company on 1 December 2006.

It is assumed that interest rates for corporation tax repayments other than by instalment remain unchanged after 14 August 2006.

X Ltd will be entitled to interest on overpaid tax, calculated as follows

		£
15.6.06 to 13.8.06	$£7,000 \times 4.25\% \times \frac{60}{365} =$	48.90
14.8.06 to 30.9.06	$£7,000 \times 4.5\% \times \frac{48}{365} =$	41.42
1.10.06 to 30.11.06	$£1,500 \times 3\% \times \frac{61}{365} =$	7.52
Total interest		£97.84

Note

(*a*)   The rate of interest on corporation tax paid early is the special higher rate applying to overpaid instalment payments (see (B) below). The special higher rate does not apply to overpaid tax after nine months after the end of the accounting period, from which date the lower normal rate applies.

(B) Repayment of tax: instalment payments [*SI 1998 No 3175* and *SI 1998 No 3176*]

Z Ltd has no associated companies and had taxable profits in excess of £1,500,000 for the year ended 31 March 2005. For the year ending 31 March 2006, Z Ltd pays £143,000 for the first instalment on 30 September 2005, this being equivalent to a quarter of its estimated corporation tax liability of £572,000. The same amount is paid on the due dates for the second and third instalments and on 5 July 2006 for the fourth instalment. On 3 September 2007, the tax liability is agreed at £506,800 and £65,200 is repaid to the company on 22 September 2007.

The rates of interest are assumed to remain unchanged after 14 August 2006.

The interest on overpaid tax is calculated as follows

Instalments due on quarter dates £506,800 $\times \frac{1}{4}$ = £126,700

	£
14 October 2005 to 13 January 2006 143,000 − 126,700 = £16,300 @ 4.25% $\times \frac{92}{365}$	174.61
14 January 2006 to 13 April 2006 286,000 − 253,400 = £32,600 @ 4.25% $\times \frac{90}{365}$	341.63
14 April 2006 to 4 July 2006 429,000 − 380,100 = £48,900 @ 4.25% $\times \frac{82}{365}$	466.89
5 July 2006 to 13 July 2006 572,000 − 380,100 = £191,900 @ 4.25% $\times \frac{9}{365}$	201.10
14 July 2006 to 13 August 2006 572,000 − 506,800 = £65,200 @ 4.25% $\times \frac{31}{365}$	235.35
14 August 2006 to 31 December 2006 572,000 − 506,800 = £65,200 @ 4.5% $\times \frac{140}{365}$	1,125.37
1 January 2007 to 21 September 2007 572,000 − 506,800 = £65,200 @ 3% $\times \frac{263}{365}$	1,409.39
Interest on overpaid tax	£3,954.34

Notes

(*a*)   Interest will not be payable before the due date of the first instalment.

(*b*)   A special higher rate of interest for instalment payments applies from the date the excess arises to the earlier of nine months after the end of the accounting period and the date the tax is repaid. Interest is calculated using the lower normal rate from the date of nine months after the end of the accounting period to the date of issue of the repayment order.

(*c*)   Debit interest works in the same way as the credit interest illustrated in this example (see 114.1(C)). For example, had Z Ltd paid less than the amount of tax due at any one of the above dates, the interest payable would be worked out on the same basis but using the relevant interest rates for unpaid tax.

113.2 **REPAYMENT ARISING FROM CARRY-BACK OF LOSSES UNDER ICTA 1988,
s 393A(1)(2)(2B): TERMINAL LOSSES**

Y Ltd prepares accounts to 31 December. It has chargeable profits of £100,000 and
£60,000 for the years to 31 December 2004 and 2005 respectively and duly pays
corporation tax of £20,250 and £12,000 on 1 October 2005 and 1 October 2006
respectively. The company ceases trading on 31 July 2006 and incurs a loss in its last
period of £80,000. It claims loss relief under *ICTA 1988, s 393A(1)(2)(2B)* against profits
of previous accounting periods. As a result of the claim, it receives a corporation tax
repayment of £16,050 on 25 July 2007 comprising £4,050 for the year to 31 December
2004 and £12,000 for the year to 31 December 2005.

Interest on overpaid tax is calculated as follows

On tax of £12,000 for year ended 31.12.05:

Date of payment	1 October 2006
Material date	1 October 2006
Interest runs from	1 October 2006

Interest runs to 25 July 2007, a total of 298 days.

On tax of £4,050 for year ended 31.12.04:

Date of payment	1 October 2005
Material date (note *(a)*)	1 May 2007
Interest runs from	1 May 2007

Interest runs to 25 July 2007, a total of 85 days.

Notes

(*a*)   Where, under a *section 393A(1)* claim, a loss is carried back to an accounting period
not falling wholly within the twelve months preceding the period of loss, the
resulting corporation tax repayment is effectively treated as a repayment of tax paid
for the period *in* which the loss is incurred, rather than for the period *to* which the
loss is carried back. [*ICTA 1988, s 826(7A); FA 1991, Sch 15 para 23; FA 1993, Sch
14 para 10(2)*].

(*b*)   HMRC use a denominator of 365 in calculations of repayment interest regardless
of whether or not a leap year is involved.

114   Interest on Unpaid Tax

114.1 **SELF-ASSESSMENT** [*FA 1998, s 32; SI 1998, No 3175; SI 1998 No 3176; SI 1999 No 1928; SI 1999 No 1929*]

(A) General

S Ltd (which has no associated companies) prepares accounts to 31 July. On 31 May 2006, it makes a payment of £80,000 in respect of its corporation tax liability for the year to 31 July 2005, the due date being 1 May 2006. On completing its corporation tax return, the company ascertains its total tax liability for the year to be £105,000 and makes a further payment of £25,000 on 16 July 2006. The final CT liability is agreed at £107,500 on 27 November 2006 and the company pays a further £2,500 on 5 January 2007.

It is assumed that the interest rates remain unchanged after 6 September 2005.

Interest on unpaid tax will be payable as follows

1.5.06 to 31.5.06	$£80,000 \times 6.5\% \times \frac{30}{366}$	=	426.23
1.5.06 to 16.7.06	$£25,000 \times 6.5\% \times \frac{76}{366}$	=	337.43
1.5.06 to 5.1.07	$£2,500 \times 6.5\% \times \frac{248}{366}$	=	110.11
Total interest charge			£873.77

Note

(*a*)   HMRC use a denominator of 366 in calculations of interest on unpaid tax regardless of whether or not a leap year is involved.

(B) Refund of interest charged

On 1 November 2006, T Ltd pays corporation tax of £100,000 for its year ended 31 December 2005. The due date for payment was 1 October 2006. The liability is finally agreed at £80,000 and a repayment of £20,000 is made to T Ltd on 1 May 2007.

The interest position will be as follows

(i)   T Ltd will be charged interest on £100,000 for the period 1.10.06 to 1.11.06 (31 days). The charge will be raised following payment of the £100,000 on 1.11.06.

$£100,000 \times 6.5\% \times \frac{31}{366} = \underline{£550.55}$

(ii)   The company will be entitled to interest on overpaid tax of £20,000 for the period 1.11.06 (date of payment) to 1.5.07 (date of repayment) (181 days).

$£20,000 \times 3\% \times \frac{181}{365} = \underline{297.53}$

(iii)   T Ltd will also receive a refund of interest charged on £20,000 for the period 1.10.06 to 1.11.06.

$£20,000 \times 6.5\% \times \frac{31}{366} = \underline{£110.11}$

114.1 Interest on Unpaid Tax

(C) Instalment payments

R Ltd has no associated companies and had taxable profits in excess of £1,500,000 for the year ended 31 March 2005. For the year ending 31 March 2006, R Ltd makes instalment payments of £110,000 (this being equivalent to a quarter of its estimated corporation tax liability of £440,000) on the first three due dates. The last instalment is not paid until 24 July 2006. On 3 September 2007, the tax liability is finally agreed at £524,800. R Ltd pays the balance due of £84,800 on 10 September 2007.

The rates of interest are assumed, for the purposes of this example, to remain unchanged after 14 August 2006.

The interest on unpaid tax is calculated as follows

Instalments due on quarter dates £524,800 × $\frac{1}{4}$ = £131,200

	£
14 October 2005 to 13 January 2006 131,200 − 110,000 = £21,200 @ 5.5% × $\frac{92}{366}$	293.09
14 January 2006 to 13 April 2006 262,400 − 220,000 = £42,400 @ 5.5% × $\frac{90}{366}$	573.44
14 April 2006 to 13 July 2006 393,600 − 330,000 = £63,600 @ 5.5% × $\frac{91}{366}$	869.72
14 July 2006 to 23 July 2006 524,800 − 330,000 = £194,800 @ 5.5% × $\frac{10}{366}$	292.73
24 July 2006 to 13 August 2006 524,800 − 440,000 = £84,800 @ 5.5% × $\frac{21}{366}$	267.61
14 August 2006 to 31 December 2006 524,800 − 440,000 = £84,800 @ 5.75% × $\frac{140}{366}$	1,865.14
1 January 2007 to 9 September 2007 524,800 − 440,000 = £84,800 @ 6.5% × $\frac{252}{366}$	3,795.15
Interest on overpaid tax	£7,956.88

Notes

(a) A special lower rate of interest for instalment payments applies from the due date of payment to the earlier of nine months after the end of the accounting period and the date the tax is paid. Interest is calculated using the higher normal rate from the date of nine months after the end of the accounting period to the date the tax is paid.

(b) Credit interest works in the same way as the debit interest illustrated in this example (see 113.1(B)). For example, had R Ltd paid more than the amount of tax due at any one of the above dates, the interest payable by HMRC would be worked out on the same basis but using the relevant interest rates for overpaid tax.

(D) Surrenders of tax refunds within a group of companies [*FA 1989, s 102*]

V Ltd has had, for some years, a 75% subsidiary, W Ltd, and both prepare accounts to 30 October. On 1 August 2006 (the due date), both companies make payments on account of their CT liabilities for the year ended 30 October 2005. V Ltd pays £250,000 and W Ltd pays £150,000. In July 2007, the liabilities are eventually agreed at £200,000 and £180,000 respectively. Before any tax repayment is made to V Ltd, the two companies jointly give notice under *FA 1989, s 102(2)* that £30,000 of the £50,000 tax repayment due to V Ltd is to be surrendered to W Ltd. W Ltd makes a payment of £20,000 to V Ltd in consideration for the tax refund surrendered.

It is assumed that the rates of interest on overdue tax and overpaid tax are, respectively, 6.5% and 3% throughout.

If no surrender had been made, and all outstanding tax payments/repayments made on, say, 1 August 2007, the interest position would have been as follows

			£
V Ltd			
Interest on CT repayment of £50,000			
for the period 1.8.06 to 1.8.07	£50,000 × 3%	=	1,500
W Ltd			
Interest on late paid CT of £30,000			
for the period 1.8.06 to 1.8.07	£30,000 × 6.5%	=	1,950
Net interest payable by the group			£450

The surrender has the following consequences

(i)   Only £20,000 of the repayment (the unsurrendered amount) is actually made, and is made to V Ltd together with interest of £600 (at 3% for 365 days).

(ii) V Ltd, the surrendering company, is treated as having received a CT repayment of £30,000 (the surrendered amount) on the 'relevant date' which in this case is the normal due date of 1.8.06, V Ltd having made its CT payment on time. V Ltd is thus not entitled to any interest on this amount.

(iii) W Ltd, the recipient company, is deemed to have paid CT of £30,000 on the 'relevant date', 1.8.06 as above. It thus incurs no interest charge.

(iv) The group has turned a net interest charge of £450 into a net interest receipt of £600, a saving of £1,050. This arises from the differential in the rates of interest charged on unpaid and overpaid tax. (The surrendered amount £30,000 × 3.5% (6.5 − 3) × 365 days = £1,050.)

(v)   The payment of £20,000 by W Ltd to V Ltd, not being a payment in excess of the surrendered refund, has no tax effect on either company.

Note

(*a*) V Ltd could have given notice to surrender its full refund of £50,000 to W Ltd, instead of just £30,000. There would, in fact, have been no point in doing so, but if W Ltd had made its original CT payment later than the due date, so as to incur an interest charge on the £150,000 originally paid, a full surrender would have produced a saving as the amount surrendered would be treated as having been paid on the due date.

115   Investment Companies and Investment Business

115.1 MANAGEMENT EXPENSES [*ICTA 1988, ss 75, 130; CAA 1990, s 28; FA 1995, Sch 8 paras 24, 57; CAA 2001, ss 18, 253; FA 2004, ss 38–47*]

XYZ Ltd, an investment company, rents out rooms, halls and equipment to conference providers. It makes up accounts to 31 March.
The following details are relevant

	31.3.03 £	31.3.04 £
Rents received	38,000	107,000
Interest receivable accrued gross	10,000	5,000
Chargeable gains	18,000	48,000
Management expenses		
attributable to property	20,000	25,000
attributable to management	50,000	40,000
Capital allowances		
attributable to property	1,000	500
attributable to management	2,000	1,000
Business charges on income	35,000	35,000

The corporation tax computations are as follows

Year ended 31.3.03

	£	£
Schedule A		
Rents		38,000
Deduct Capital allowances	1,000	
Management expenses	20,000	(21,000)
		17,000
Schedule D, Case III		10,000
Chargeable gains		18,000
		45,000
Deduct Management expenses	50,000	
Capital allowances	2,000	(52,000)
		(7,000)
Deduct Business charges		(35,000)
Unrelieved balance carried forward		£(42,000)

Year ended 31.3.04

	£	£
Schedule A		
Rents		107,000
Deduct Capital allowances	500	
Management expenses	25,000	(25,500)
		81,500
Schedule D, Case III		5,000
Chargeable gains		48,000
		c/f £134,500

	£	£
		b/f 134,500
Deduct Management expenses	40,000	
Capital allowances	1,000	
Unrelieved balance from		
previous accounting period	42,000	(83,000)
		51,500
Deduct Business charges		(35,000)
Profit chargeable to CT		£16,500

On 1 April 2004, XYZ Ltd diversified and began to provide conference services itself.

The following details are relevant for the year ending 31 March 2007.

	31.3.07
	£
Income from conferences	65,000
Rents received	40,000
Interest receivable accrued (gross)	5,000
Conference costs	22,000
Management expenses	
attributable to property	20,000
attributable to management	73,000
Capital allowances	
attributable to conferences	2,000
attributable to property	400
attributable to management	800

The corporation tax computations are as follows.

Year ended 31.3.07

	£	£	£
Schedule D			
Trading income			65,000
Deduct Conference costs		22,000	
Capital allowances		2,000	
			(24,000)
			41,000
Schedule A			
Rents		40,000	
Deduct Capital allowances	400		
Management expenses	20,000	(20,400)	
			19,600
Schedule D, Case III			5,000
Deduct Management expenses	73,000		
Capital allowances	800		
			(73,800)
Unrelieved balance carried forward			£(8,200)

115.1 Investment Companies and Investment Business

Notes

(a) For accounting periods beginning on or after 1 April 2004, relief for management expenses is extended to companies with investment business whether or not they qualify as investment companies. Under the new rules, management expenses are deductible for corporation tax purposes for the accounting period in which they are charged to the accounts whereas under the former rules, they were allowable when 'disbursed' although in practice, HMRC have generally accepted the former procedure. There are transitional provisions dealing with this change for management expenses carried forward and with accounting periods straddling 1 April 2004. [*ICTA 1988, ss 75–75B; FA 2004, ss 38–47*]. A company with investment business is defined as 'any company whose business consists wholly or partly in the making of investments'. [*ICTA 1988, s 130; FA 2004, s 38(2)–(5)*]. (It will include, for example, a trading company with shares in subsidiary companies.)

(b) The profits of a company's 'Schedule A business' are computed, broadly, in the same way as the profits of a trade are computed for the purposes of Case I of Schedule D. [*ICTA 1988, ss 15, 21–42A; FA 1998, ss 38–41, Sch 5*]. It is necessary to distinguish expenses of a general management nature from those pertaining to properties etc.

(c) The excess management expenses (including capital allowances) in the accounting period ended 31.3.03 are carried forward to the accounting period ended 31.3.04 and are set against total profits of that period. If profits in the year ended 31.3.04 had been insufficient, the excess management expenses could have been carried forward to subsequent periods until fully used. Similarly, the excess management expenses in the accounting period ended 31.3.07 can be carried forward to subsequent accounting periods. See also note (e) below.

(d) Management expenses brought forward from earlier accounting periods cannot be included in a group relief claim. [*ICTA 1988, s 403ZD(4); FA 1998, Sch 5 para 29*].

(e) Surplus management expenses may not be carried forward if there is a change of ownership of an investment company and one of the following occurs:

    (i) a significant increase (as defined) in the company's capital after the change of ownership,

    (ii) a major change in the nature or conduct of the business of the company in the period beginning three years before the change and ending three years after,

    (iii) a considerable revival of the company's business which before the change was small or negligible.

[*ICTA 1988, ss 768B, 768C, Sch 28A*].

116 Liquidation

116.1 ACCOUNTING PERIODS IN A LIQUIDATION [*ICTA 1988, ss 12(7), 342*]
On 31 August 2003 a resolution was passed to wind up X Ltd. The company's normal accounting date was 31 December.

It was later agreed between the liquidator and the Inspector that 31 January 2006 would be the assumed date of completion of winding-up. The actual date of completion is 30 April 2007.

The last accounting period of the company before liquidation is
1.1.04 to 31.8.04   —   8 months

The accounting periods during the liquidation are as follows
1.9.04 to 31.8.05   —   12 months
1.9.05 to 31.1.06   —   5 months
1.2.06 to 31.1.07   —   12 months
1.2.07 to 30.4.07   —   3 months

Notes

(*a*) The final and penultimate financial years for the above accounting periods are 2007 and 2006 respectively. Assuming the small companies rate of CT is applicable for all financial years concerned, the rate of 19% applies to the income of financial year 2006. If the rate for the financial year in which the winding-up is completed has not been fixed or proposed by Budget resolution before completion of the winding-up, the rate for the preceding financial year will apply to the income of that year.

(*b*) If the company is a close company, it may be unable, following the commencement of winding-up, to comply with *ICTA 1988, s 13A(2)*. It would then be a close investment-holding company (CIC) and liable to the full rate of corporation tax whatever the level of profits. This does not apply to the accounting period beginning on commencement of the winding-up providing the company was not a CIC for the accounting period immediately before the commencement of the winding-up; however, a company which had ceased to trade before commencement of winding-up is unlikely to be able to satisfy this condition. [*ICTA 1988, ss 13(1)(b), 13A; FA 1989, s 105; FA 1999, s 28(2)(7)*].

117   Loan Relationships

117.1 TRADING PURPOSE [*FA 1996, ss 80, 81, 82, 84–85B*]

A Ltd requires additional trade finance and on 1 January 2006 enters into an agreement with XY Bank plc to borrow £100,000 for 3 years. Interest is payable every 6 months commencing 1 July 2006 at 6% per annum. Legal fees and negotiation expenses in respect of this loan paid in December 2005 amount to £2,800. The company's accounting reference date is 31 March and it adopts an authorised accruals basis for all loan relationships.

A Ltd's accounts for the year ended 31 March 2006 show the following

	£	£
Turnover		1,400,000
Purchases and expenses		
(all allowable for corporation tax purposes)	900,000	
Finance Charges		
XY Bank plc – interest to 31 March 2006	1,500	
Legal fees and negotiation expenses	2,800	
Depreciation*	120,000	
		1,024,300
Net profit per accounts		£375,700

* Capital allowances for the same year are £95,000.

The company's corporation tax computation for the same period is as follows

	£
Net profit per accounts	375,700
Add: Depreciation	120,000
Less: Capital allowances	(95,000)
Adjusted profit for corporation tax purposes	£400,700

For corporation tax purposes the accrued interest on the loan with XY Bank plc taken out for trading purposes will be treated as a trading expense.

The profit and loss charge for each of the following accounting periods will be

	Year ended 31.3.06	Year ended 31.3.07	Year ended 31.3.08	Year ended 31.3.09
	£	£	£	£
'Debits'				
Expenses	2,800	—	—	—
Interest payable	1,500	6,000	6,000	4,500

This conforms to the amortised cost basis of accounting as interest will be allocated to the period to which it relates.

Notes

(a)   A company has a loan relationship whenever it stands in the position of debtor or creditor in respect of a money debt. (A money debt being any debt not arising in the normal course of purchase and sale of goods and services for resale.) [*FA 1996, s 81*].

(b)   The taxation of the loan relationship follows accounts drawn up in accordance with generally accepted accounting practice, using either an amortised cost basis or fair value basis of accounting (broadly for periods of account beginning before 1 January 2005 known as an authorised accounting method (either authorised accruals or mark to market) — see note (b) in 117.2 below). [*FA 1996, ss 85A, 85B (FA 1996, s 85); FA 2004, s 52, Sch 10 para 3*].

(c)   Interest payments on current loans for trading purposes are treated as a trading expense. [*FA 1996, s 82*].

117.2 NON-TRADING PURPOSES

Tradissimo Ltd, a trading company, bought £10,000 nominal of gilt edged securities at £94 per £100 nominal stock as a speculative venture on 1 January 2005. The gilts will be redeemed on 1 January 2008 at par. Interest at 5% is payable annually on 31 December each year. The company uses the authorised accruals accounting method for all its loan relationships. The accounting reference date is 31 March.

As the purchase of the gilt-edged security does not relate to the company's trade, its income and expenditure will be assessed under Schedule D, Case III. In addition to the interest the company will also be taxable on the discount which will be spread over three years.

	Year ended 31.3.05 £	Year ended 31.3.06 £	Year ended 31.3.07 £	Year ended 31.3.08 £
'Credits'				
Interest received	125	500	500	375
Discount	50	200	200	150
Schedule D, Case III	£175	£700	£700	£525

Notes

(a)   Profits and losses from non-trading loan relationships are taxable under Schedule D, Case III. [*FA 1996, s 80(3)*].

(b)   For periods of account beginning on or after 1 January 2005 (or any period of account beginning before that date in which international accounting standards are required or permitted to be adopted in the preparation of the company's accounts) profits or losses arising from the loan relationship are to be based on the company accounts prepared in accordance with UK generally accepted accounting practice or international accounting standards. Previously, all profits and losses arising from the loan relationship were to be accounted for using the authorised accruals basis. [*FA 1996, ss 84, 85A, 85B; FA 2004, s 52, Sch 10 paras 1, 3*].

117.3 Loan Relationships

117.3 **NON-TRADING DEFICIT ON A LOAN RELATIONSHIP** [*FA 1996, s 83, Sch 8*]
The Beta Trading Co Ltd, which is a single company and not part of a group, made a loan to the PQR Company Ltd. This transaction did not form part of Beta's normal trade. PQR Company Ltd defaults on the loan on 1 October 2005 leaving a balance of £8,500 due to The Beta Trading Co Ltd. The accounting reference date is 31 March.

The Beta Trading Co Ltd's computations for relevant years are as follows

	Year ended 31.3.04 £	Year ended 31.3.05 £	Year ended 31.3.06 £	Year ended 31.3.07 £
Schedule D, Case I (trading income)	10,000	11,000	800	12,000
Schedule D, Case III (non-trading loan relationship income)	2,000	2,000	100	400

The £8,500 debit is set against the non-trading loan relationship credit of £100 in the year ending 31 March 2006 and the remaining deficit of £8,400 may be relieved in whole or in part in three different ways (group relief not being available).

	£
Non-trading deficit	8,400
1. Set off against total profits of the year ended 31 March 2006	(800)
2. Carry back against Schedule D, Case III profits from non-trading loan relationships of the preceding accounting period	(2,000)
3. Carry forward against non-trading profits of the company for year ended 31 March 2007	(400)
Net deficit to carry forward against subsequent non-trading profits	£5,200

Notes

(*a*) For accounting periods beginning before 1 October 2002 (i.e. the above period ending 31 March 2002), relief was provided by claim for a non-trading deficit on a loan relationship by one of the four following methods:

   (i) by set off against any profits of the company of whatever description for the deficit period,

   (ii) to be treated as eligible for group relief,

   (iii) to be carried back to be set off against profits for earlier accounting periods, or

   (iv) to be carried forward and set against non-trading profits for the next accounting period. [*FA 1996, s 83(2), Sch 8*].

(*b*) For accounting periods beginning on or after 1 October 2002, relief for a non-trading deficit may be claimed (to the extent not already surrendered as group relief, for which a separate claim is no longer required) either:

   (i) by set-off against profits of the company of whatever description for the deficit period; or

   (ii) by carry back and set-off against profits of the preceding accounting period arising from non-trading loan relationships.

(*c*) Where relief is not claimed as in (*b*) above, the non-trading deficit is automatically carried forward for set-off against non-trading profits of the subsequent accounting period, subject to a claim for it to be not so carried forward, in which case it is treated as a non-trading deficit of that period to be carried forward for offset against non-trading profits of succeeding accounting periods.

(d)   The £5,200 deficit balance (which profits for the year ended 31 March 2007 are insufficient to relieve) will be carried forward for relief against non-trading profits of the next and subsequent accounting periods subject to a claim as in (c) above. [FA 1996, s 83(3A)].

117.4 FOREIGN EXCHANGE AND LATE PAID INTEREST

[FA 1996, ss 84A, 87, 103(1A)(1B), Sch 9 para 2; FA 2002, Sch 26 para 14(3)]

On 1 October 2004, Subco Ltd, a UK trading company preparing accounts to 30 September, obtains a three-year loan of US $850,000 from its parent company to finance the purchase of plant. Interest on the loan is payable at an annual rate of 5% at the end of every six months. The first interest payment is made on the due date on 31 March 2005 and the interest due is accrued thereafter but no further payments are made, due to Subco's financial difficulties, until 31 March 2007. Also on 1 October 2004, Subco bought a forward currency contract of $850,000 for delivery on 30 September 2007 in order to repay the loan.

Assume that the exchange rates and sterling amounts at the relevant dates are:

Date	$ to £	£ equivalent of loan	Interest paid – £	Interest accrued – £
1.10.04	1.85	459,459		
31.3.05	1.90		11,184	
30.9.05	1.70	500,000		12,500
30.9.06	1.85	459,459		22,973
31.3.07	1.90		44,737	
30.9.07	1.85	459,459	11,486	

The cost of the forward currency contract gives rise to allowable debits of £15,000 per year, calculated on an amortised cost basis of accounting (see note (b) to 117.2 above).

The company incurs the following loan relationship credits and debits.

Year ending	30.9.05 £	30.9.06 £	30.9.07 £
Non-trading debits:			
Interest	11,184	22,973	33,854
Non-trading derivative contract debits	15,000	15,000	15,000
Total loan relationship debits	(26,184)	(37,973)	(48,854)
Exchange gains (losses) on loan	(40,541)	40,541	—
Exchange gain on interest*	.		605
Non-trading loan relationship profit		2,568	
Non-trading loan relationship deficit	(66,725)		(48,249)

* £22,973 – £22,368 ($42,500/1.90) = £605

Notes

(a)   Where the parties to the loan relationship are 'connected' under FA 1996, s 87 and an amortised cost basis of accounting is used (see note (b) to 117.2 above), the debits relating to the interest payable under the relationship are not brought into account until the interest is paid where:

(i)   the interest is not paid within twelve months of the end of the accounting period in which it would otherwise accrue; and

(ii) the interest receipts are not brought into accounts as loan relationship credits for any accounting period by the loan relationship creditor. [*FA 1996, Sch 9 paras 2, 20*].

Interest payable on 30.9.05 of $21,250 is not paid by 30.9.06 and so the debit cannot be accounted for until the accounting period in which it is paid, the year ending 30.9.07. The interest which would under the amortised cost basis be accounted for in the year ending 30.9.06 is paid within twelve months of that date and accordingly, is deductible in that period.

(b)   Under the derivative contracts rules, non-trading credits or debits arising from derivative contracts are treated as if they were non-trading loan relationship debits or credits and effectively aggregated with other non-trading loan relationship debits or credits, the net amount being chargeable under Schedule D, Case III or relievable as a non-trading deficit. [*FA 2002, Sch 26 para 14(3)*].

(c)   The rules for the taxation of foreign exchange gains and losses, introduced by *FA 1993*, were assimilated by *FA 2002* into the rules for loan relationships and derivative contracts for accounting periods beginning on or after 1 October 2002. Accordingly, from that date, loan relationship debits and credits are computed so as to include any related exchange gains or losses apart from gains and losses taken to and sustained by a company reserve under the matching rules (which are ignored for the purposes of this example). [*FA 1996, ss 84A, 87, 103(1A)(1B)* (as amended by *FA 2004, s 52, Sch 10 paras 2,4*)].

118   Losses

118.1   CURRENT YEAR SET-OFF OF TRADING LOSSES [*ICTA 1988, s 393A(1)(a); FA 1991, s 73*]

A Ltd is a trading company with investment business (see 115.1 INVESTMENT COMPANIES AND INVESTMENT BUSINESS). Its results for the year ended 31 March 2007 show

	£
Trading loss	(10,000)
Schedule A	3,000
Schedule D, Case III	4,000
Chargeable gains	7,200
Management expenses	(2,000)
Qualifying charitable donations	(1,000)

The loss may be relieved as follows

	£
Schedule A	3,000
Schedule D, Case III	4,000
Chargeable gains	7,200
	14,200
Deduct Management expenses	(2,000)
	12,200
Deduct Trading loss	(10,000)
	2,200
Deduct Qualifying charitable donations	(1,000)
Profits chargeable to CT	£1,200
CT payable at 0%	Nil

Note

(a)   Loss relief (other than group relief) against profits for the current year is given in priority to qualifying charitable donations which are treated as non-trade charges. [*ICTA 1988, s 338(1)*]. See 121.2 PROFIT COMPUTATIONS for treatment of excess charges.

118.2   CARRY-FORWARD OF TRADING LOSSES [*ICTA 1988, ss 338(1), 393(1)(9), 393A(1)(a); FA 1990, s 99(2)*]

B Ltd has carried on the same trade for many years. The results for the years ended 30 September 2005, 2006 and 2007 are shown below

	2005	2006	2007
	£	£	£
Trading profit/(loss)	(20,000)	10,000	5,000
Schedule A	3,000	1,000	2,000
Schedule D, Case III	2,000	2,000	3,000
Chargeable gains	5,600	4,700	4,000
Trade charges (note (a))	(3,000)	—	—
Management expenses	—	(9,000)	—

118.2 Losses

B Ltd may claim under *ICTA 1988, s 393A(1)(a)* to set off the trading loss against other profits of the same accounting period. Assuming the claim is made (and that no claim is made to carry back the balance of the loss), the loss will be set off as follows

Year ended 30 September 2005	£	Loss memorandum £
Trading loss		(20,000)
Schedule A	3,000	
Schedule D, Case III	2,000	
Chargeable gains	5,600	
	10,600	
Deduct Trading loss	(10,600)	10,600
	—	(9,400)
Trade charges	—	(3,000)
Profits chargeable to CT	—	
		(12,400)

Year ended 30 September 2006		
Schedule D, Case I	10,000	
Deduct Loss brought forward	(10,000)	10,000
	—	(2,400)
Schedule A	1,000	
Schedule D, Case III	2,000	
Chargeable gains	4,700	
	7,700	
Deduct Management expenses (restricted)	(7,700)	
Profits chargeable to CT	—	
Management expenses carried forward	£1,300	

Year ended 30 September 2007		
Schedule D, Case I	5,000	
Deduct Loss brought forward	(2,400)	2,400
	2,600	
Schedule A	2,000	
Schedule D, Case III	3,000	
Chargeable gains	4,000	
	11,600	
Deduct Management expenses	(1,300)	
Profits chargeable to CT	10,300	

Note

(a)   The trade charges are paid before 16 March 2005. Thereafter they are treated as management expenses. See 121.2 PROFIT COMPUTATIONS, note (b).

118.3 **CARRY-BACK OF TRADING LOSSES** [*ICTA 1988, s 393A(1)(2)(2A)(2B)(8); FA 1991, s 73*]

(A) Terminal losses
X Ltd has the following results for the two years ending 31 December 2004 and 2005 and its final period to 30 September 2006 when it ceases trading.

	31.12.04 £	31.12.05 £	30.9.06 £
Trading profit/(loss)	30,000	4,500	(30,000)
Schedule A	1,000	1,000	3,000
Schedule D, Case III	500	500	4,000
Chargeable gains	—	1,500	2,250
Trade charges	(4,000)	(2,000)	—
Management expenses	—	(2,000)	(4,000)
Non-trade charges	—	(1,000)	—

The loss can be relieved as follows

	£	£	Loss memorandum £
Period ended 30 September 2006			
Trading loss			(30,000)
Schedule A		3,000	
Schedule D, Case III		4,000	
Chargeable gains		2,250	
		9,250	
Deduct Management expenses		(4,000)	
Trading loss (*ICTA 1988, s 393A(1)(a)*)		(5,250)	5,250
Profits chargeable to CT		—	
			(24,750)
Year ended 31 December 2005			
Schedule D, Case I		4,500	
Schedule A		1,000	
Schedule D, Case III		500	
Chargeable gains		1,500	
		7,500	
Deduct Management expenses		(2,000)	
Trade charges (note (*b*))		(2,000)	
		3,500	
Deduct Loss carried back (*ICTA 1988, s 393A(1)(b)(2A)(2B)*)		(3,500)	3,500
Profits chargeable to CT		—	
Unrelieved non-trade charges	(1,000)		
			c/f £(21,250)

118.3 Losses

	£	£
		b/f (21,250)

Year ended 31 December 2004

	£	£
Schedule D, Case I	30,000	
Schedule A	1,000	
Schedule D, Case III	500	
	31,500	
Deduct Trade charges	(4,000)	
	27,500	
Deduct Loss carried back (*ICTA 1988, s 393A(1)(b)(2A)(2B)*)	21,250	21,250
Profits chargeable to CT	£6,250	
Losses remaining (note (*a*))		—

Notes

(*a*)   Where a loss is incurred in the accounting period in which the trade is discontinued, it may be carried back for three years prior to the period in which the loss occurred. In this example, the losses are fully utilised in the year ended 31 December 2004 but if this were not the case, they could have been carried back to the year ended 31 December 2003. Similar relief is available where the loss is incurred in an accounting period ending within the 12 months immediately before the cessation but in this case the three year carry-back is limited to an apportioned part of the loss for that penultimate period. This apportionment is on a time basis, by reference to the proportion of the accounting period falling within the final 12-month period. The balance attributable to the earlier part of the accounting period can be carried back one year in the normal way. [*ICTA 1998, s 393A(2)(2A)(2B)*].

(*b*)   Trade charges (but not non-trade charges) are relieved in priority to losses carried back from a later accounting period. [*ICTA 1988, s 393A(8); FA 1991, s 73*]. In determining terminal losses, excess trade charges (to the extent they exceed any profits from which they may be deducted) are treated as trading expenses in the period. No relief is available for the non-trade charges for the year to 31 December 2004 in this example, as they can be carried neither forward nor back. Payments made on or after 16 March 2005 which would have been treated as trade charges before that date (such as annuities) are deductible as management expenses (subject to transitional provisions) where they meet the requirements for such expenses. [*F(No 2) A 2005, s 38*]. (See 121.2 PROFIT COMPUTATIONS.)

(*c*)   Trading losses may be carried back only one year. Losses must be set against current year profits before being carried back. If carried back, they must be carried back to the full extent possible, i.e. if losses are not fully relieved in the immediately preceding period, any balance must then be carried back to the period before that, and so on. [*ICTA 1988, s 393A(1)(2)*].

(B) Accounting periods of different lengths

Y Ltd, which previously made up accounts to 31 March, changed its accounting date to 31 December. Its results for the three accounting periods up to 31 December 2006 were as follows

	12 months 31.3.05 £	9 months 31.12.05 £	12 months 31.12.06 £
Trading profit/ (loss)	5,500	9,000	(66,000)
Schedule D, Case III	2,500	3,000	—
Chargeable gains	—	—	2,000

Y Ltd makes all available loss relief claims so as to obtain relief against the earliest possible profits.

The computations are summarised as follows

	12 months 31.3.05 £	9 months 31.12.05 £	12 months 31.12.06 £
Schedule D, Case I	5,500	9,000	—
Schedule D, Case III	2,500	3,000	—
Chargeable gains	—	—	2,000
	8,000	12,000	2,000
Loss relief			
ICTA 1988, s 393A(1)(a)			(2,000)
ICTA 1988, s 393A(1)(b)	(2,000)	(12,000)	
Profits chargeable to CT	£6,000	—	—

Loss memoranda

	12 months 31.12.05 £
Trading loss	66,000
Relieved against current year profits	(2,000)
Relieved by carry-back:	
To p/e 31.12.05	(12,000)
To y/e 31.3.05	(2,000)
Carried forward under ICTA 1988, s 393(1)	£50,000

Note

(a)   Relief under ICTA 1988, s 393A(1)(b) (carry-back of losses) is not restricted by reference to the length of the accounting period of loss. However, where a loss is carried back to an accounting period falling partly outside the carry-back period, relief is restricted to an appropriate proportion of profits. [ICTA 1988, s 393A(2)]. In this example, the one-year period, as regards the loss for the year to 31 December 2006, begins on 1 January 2005 and, therefore, only three-twelfths of the profit for the year to 31 March 2005 can be relieved.

118.4   Losses

LOSSES ON UNLISTED SHARES [*ICTA 1988, ss 573, 575, 576*]

Z Ltd has been an investment company since its incorporation in 1972. It is not part of a trading group and has no associated companies. It makes up accounts to 31 December. On 6 February 2006, Z Ltd disposed of part of its holding of shares in T Ltd for full market value. Z Ltd makes no global re-basing election under *TCGA 1992, s 35(5)*.

Details of disposal

Contract date	6.2.06
Shares sold	2,000 Ord
Proceeds (after expenses)	£4,500

Z acquired its shares in T Ltd as follows

				£
6.4.80 subscribed for	1,000 shares	cost (with expenses)		5,000
6.4.90 acquired	1,500 shares	cost (with expenses)		4,000
	2,500			£9,000

T Ltd shares were valued at £3 per share at 31 March 1982. T Ltd has been a UK resident trading company since 1980. Its shares are not quoted on a recognised stock exchange.

Z Ltd may claim that part of the loss incurred be set off against its income as follows

Identification on last in, first out basis

(i)   Shares acquired 6.4.90 (not subscribed for)

	£
Proceeds of 1,500 shares	
$\dfrac{1{,}500}{2{,}000} \times £4{,}500$	3,375
Cost of 1,500 shares	(4,000)
Capital loss *not* available for set-off against income	£(625)

(ii)   Shares acquired 6.4.80 (subscribed for)

	Cost basis £	31.3.82 value basis £
Proceeds of 500 shares		
$\dfrac{500}{2{,}000} \times £4{,}500$	1,125	1,125
Cost of 500 shares	(2,500)	
31.3.82 value		(1,500)
	£(1,375)	£(375)
Capital loss available for set-off against income		£(375)

Notes

(*a*)   A claim under *ICTA 1988, s 573* is restricted to the loss in respect of the shares *subscribed* for.

(*b*)   The claim must be submitted within two years of the end of the accounting period in which the loss was incurred.

(*c*)   The loss of £375 is available primarily against income of the year ended 31 December 2006, with any balance being available against, broadly speaking, income of the 12 months ended 31 December 2005.

(*d*)   See IT 13.5 LOSSES and CGT 216.3 LOSSES for further examples on this topic.

118.5 Losses

118.5 **RESTRICTION OF TRADING LOSSES ON RECONSTRUCTION WITHOUT CHANGE OF OWNERSHIP** [*ICTA 1988, ss 343, 344*]

(A) Transfer of trade

A Ltd and B Ltd are two wholly-owned subsidiaries of X Ltd. All are within the charge to corporation tax, although A Ltd has accumulated trading losses brought forward and unrelieved of £200,000 and has not paid tax for several years. As part of a group reorganisation, A Ltd's trade is transferred to B Ltd on 31 October 2006.

A Ltd's balance sheet immediately before the transfer is as follows

	£		£
Share capital	100,000	Property	90,000
Debenture secured		Plant	20,000
on property	50,000	Stock	130,000
Group loan	10,000	Trade debtors	120,000
Trade creditors	300,000		
Bank overdraft	60,000		
	520,000		
Deficit on			
reserves	(160,000)		
	£360,000		£360,000

Book values represent the approximate open market values of assets. B Ltd takes over the stock and plant to continue the trade, paying £150,000 to A Ltd and taking over £15,000 of trade creditors relating to stock. A Ltd is to collect outstanding debts and pay remaining creditors.

A Ltd's 'relevant assets' are

	£
Freehold property (£90,000 − £50,000)	40,000
Trade debtors	120,000
Consideration from B Ltd	150,000
	£310,000

A Ltd's 'relevant liabilities' are

	£
Bank overdraft	60,000
Group loan	10,000
Trade creditors (£300,000 − £15,000)	285,000
	£355,000

Tax losses transferable with trade
£200,000 − £(355,000 − 310,000) = £155,000

Notes

(*a*) Assets taken over by the successor to the trade are not included in relevant assets. Loan stock is not a relevant liability, but where the loan is secured on an asset which is not transferred, the value of the asset is reduced by the amount secured.

(*b*) The assumption by B Ltd of liability for £15,000 of trade creditors does not constitute the giving of consideration and is not, therefore, a relevant asset of A Ltd. A Ltd's relevant liabilities are, however, reduced by the amount taken over.

(B) Transfer of part of a trade

D Ltd and E Ltd are wholly-owned subsidiaries of X Ltd. On 1 November 2006 D Ltd transfers the manufacturing part of what has been an integrated trade to E Ltd. D Ltd has accumulated trading losses brought forward and unrelieved of £150,000, of which £50,000 are attributable to the manufacturing operations.

Immediately before the transfer D Ltd's balance sheet is as follows

	£		£
Share capital	100,000	Property — shops	110,000
Share premium	18,000	factory	70,000
Loan stock	50,000	Plant	45,000
Trade creditors	290,000	Vehicles	20,000
Bank overdraft	42,000	Stock	30,000
		Trade debtors	65,000
	500,000		
Deficit on			
reserves	(160,000)		
	£340,000		£340,000

Book values represent the approximate open market value of assets. E Ltd takes over the manufacturing business together with the factory, plant and £18,000 of stock for a total consideration of £134,000.

Approximately 60% of D Ltd's turnover relates to manufacturing, and it is agreed that trade debtors and creditors are proportional to turnover.

D Ltd's 'relevant assets' apportioned to the trade transferred are

	£
Trade debtors (60%)	39,000
Consideration received from E Ltd	134,000
	£173,000

'Relevant liabilities' apportioned to the trade are

	£
Trade creditors (60%)	174,000
Overdraft (33%) note (a)	14,000
	£188,000

Tax losses transferable are restricted to
£50,000 − £(188,000 − 173,000) = £35,000

Notes

(a) On the transfer of part of a trade, such apportionments of receipts, expenses, assets or liabilities shall be made as may be just. It is assumed that it is reasonable to apportion trade debtors and creditors in proportion to turnover and the overdraft in proportion to losses.

(b) Loan stock, share premium and share capital are not relevant liabilities unless they have arisen in replacing relevant liabilities within the preceding year.

(c) If the trade were transferred as a whole for market value of the assets, no restriction would apply to the losses transferable.

118.6 Losses

118.6 **SCHEDULE A LOSSES** [*ICTA 1988, s 392A*]

JW Ltd, an investment company, has the following results for the three years ended 30 April 2007:

	y/e 30.4.05	y/e 30.4.06	y/e 30.4.07
	£	£	£
Schedule D, Case III	6,000	6,000	6,000
Schedule A profit/(loss)	(7,500)	2,000	(8,500)
Management expenses	300	300	500

In view of the continuing losses, JW Ltd closes down its Schedule A business on 30 April 2007. It sells its properties in the year ended 30 April 2008, realising chargeable gains of £155,000. The company has Schedule D, Case III income for that year of £6,000 and incurs management expenses of £600.

The company's profits chargeable to corporation tax for the four years are as follows.

	£	£
y/e 30.4.05		
Schedule D, Case III		6,000
Deduct management expenses	300	
Schedule A loss (restricted)	5,700	6,000
Profits chargeable to CT		Nil
y/e 30.4.06		
Schedule D, Case III		6,000
Schedule A		2,000
		8,000
Deduct management expenses	300	
Schedule A loss (y/e 30.4.05)	1,800	2,100
Profits chargeable to CT		£5,900
y/e 30.4.07		
Schedule D, Case III		6,000
Deduct management expenses	500	
Schedule A loss (restricted)	5,500	6,000
Profits chargeable to CT		Nil
y/e 30.4.08		
Schedule D, Case III		6,000
Chargeable gains		155,000
		161,000
Deduct management expenses		3,600
Profits chargeable to CT		£157,400

Loss memorandum	£
Loss for y/e 30.4.05	7,500
Used y/e 30.4.05	5,700
Used y/e 30.4.06	1,800
	Nil

	£
Loss for y/e 30.4.07	8,500
Used y/e 30.4.07	5,500
Carried forward as management expenses (relieved y/e 30.4.08)	£3,000

Notes

(a)   Relief for Schedule A losses is only available where the Schedule A business is carried on as a commercial business or in the exercise of a statutory function.

(b)   As A Ltd is an investment company, on ceasing the Schedule A business, the unrelieved losses of £3,000 are treated as excess management expenses. [*ICTA 1988, s 392A(3)*].

119 Non-Corporate Distribution Rate

119.1 **BASIC PROFITS MATCHING NON-CORPORATE DISTRIBUTIONS** [*ICTA 1988, s 13AB, Sch A2 paras 2, 3; FA 2004, s 28, Sch 3; FA 2006, s 26*]

In its accounting period ending 31 March 2006, A Ltd makes a profit chargeable to corporation tax of £9,500 and distributes the same amount to the sole shareholder, Mr X.

The company's basic profits are taxable at the corporation tax starting rate of 0% and thus the effective underlying tax rate is 0%. However, the basic profits match the non-corporate distribution of £9,500 and an amount equal to the NCDs is therefore taxed at the non-corporate distribution rate of 19% resulting in corporation tax due of £1,805.

Notes

(a) For distributions made after 31 March 2004 and before 1 April 2006, a special rate (set at 19% (the small companies' rate) for the financial year 2004), the '*non-corporate distribution rate*', applies where a company, which has an underlying rate of corporation tax of less than that rate, makes (or is treated as making) one or more 'non-corporate distributions' (NCDs) (broadly to persons other than companies) in any accounting period. Where an accounting period straddles 1 April 2004 or 1 April 2006 the accounting periods falling in the different financial years are treated as separate accounting periods and the profits are apportioned between the two periods pro rata on a time basis unless that method produces an unjust or unreasonable result in which case the profits are to be apportioned using a just and reasonable method. Only the profits from 1 April 2004 and before 1 April 2006 are considered for the purposes of the NCD rate.

(b) The 19% rate is applied to the amount of the company's basic profits of an accounting period that matches the NCDs and the company's underlying rate of tax is applied to the remainder (see 119.2 below).

119.2 **BASIC PROFITS EXCEEDING NON-CORPORATE DISTRIBUTIONS** [*ICTA 1988, s 13AB, Sch A2 paras 2–4; FA 2004, s 28, Sch 3; FA 2006, s 26*]
AB Ltd is owned 80% by Mr X and 20% by Z Ltd and has no associated companies. In its accounting period ending 31 March 2006, AB Ltd makes a profit chargeable to corporation tax of £45,000. In the same period, the company pays dividends of £20,000 to Mr X and £5000 to Z Ltd. AB Ltd's corporation tax is computed as follows.

		£
Profits chargeable to corporation tax		45,000
Corporation tax @ 19%		8,550.00
Less: marginal relief:	(£50,000 – £45,000) x 19/400	237.50
Underlying corporation tax due		8,312.50
Underlying rate	(£8,312.50/£45,000) x 100	18.47%
Non-corporate distribution	£20,000 @ 19%	3,800.00
Remaining profits at under-lying rate	£25,000 @ 18.47%	4,617.50
Total corporation tax due		£8,417.50

Notes
(*a*)   Where the distributions made (or treated as made) in an accounting period do not exceed the company's basic profits the 19% rate is effectively applied to the amount of the NCDs made and the effective underlying rate is applied to the remaining profits.

(*b*)   Where the distributions exceed the company's basic profits the 19% rate is applied to that proportion of basic profits that the NCDs bear to total distributions, the company's underlying tax rate applying to the remainder (see 119.3 below).

(*c*)   See also note (*a*) at 119.1 above.

119.3   Non-Corporate Distribution Rate

119.3   NON-CORPORATE DISTRIBUTIONS EXCEEDING BASIC PROFITS [*ICTA 1988, s 13AB, Sch A2 paras 5, 6, 13; FA 2004, s 28, Sch 3; FA 2006, s 26*]
ABC Ltd is owned 80% by Mr P and 20% by Q Ltd and has no associated companies. In its accounting period ending 30 September 2005, ABC Ltd makes a profit chargeable to corporation tax of £20,000. On 30 September 2005, the company pays dividends from its reserves of £20,000 to Mr P and £5,000 to Q Ltd. ABC Ltd's corporation tax is computed as follows.

		£
Profits chargeable to corporation tax		20,000
Corporation tax @ 19%		3,800
Less: marginal relief:	(£50,000 − £20,000) × 19/400	1,425
Underlying corporation tax due		2,375
Underlying rate	(£2,375/£20,000) × 100	11.875%
Non-corporate distributions	£16,000 @ 19% (note (*a*))	3,040.00
Remaining profits at under-		
lying rate	£4,000 @ 11.875%	475.00
Total corporation tax due		£3,515.00

Notes

(*a*)   Where the distributions exceed the company's basic profits the 19% rate is applied to that proportion of basic profits that the NCDs bear to total distributions, the company's underlying tax rate applying to the remainder. The total distributions of £25,000 exceed these basic profits so only 80% (NCDs £20,000 / total distributions £25,000 = 80%) of the profits, i.e. £16,000 (80% × £20,000) are matched with the NCDs.

(*b*)   The amount by which NCDs exceed the amount of matching basic profits for a period ('*excess NCDs*') must, in certain circumstances, be allocated to another company in which case the recipient company is treated as if it had made the NCD in the period to which it is allocated (see 119.4 below). Since the excess NCDs of £4,000 cannot be allocated to another company, they are carried forward to the next accounting period and are treated as having been made (in addition to any distributions actually made) in ABC Ltd's next accounting period.

(*c*)   See also note (*a*) at 119.1 above.

119.4 **ALLOCATION TO GROUP COMPANIES** [*ICTA 1988, s 13AB, Sch A2 paras 6, 7, 13, 14, 17, 18; FA 2004, s 28, Sch 3; FA 2006, s 26*].

J Ltd is owned 80% by Mr T and 20% by Z Ltd. During its accounting period ending 31 December 2005, it receives no income other than a distribution of £15,000 from its 75% subsidiary, K Ltd. J Ltd distributes £12,000 to Mr T and £3,000 to Z Ltd on 31 December 2005. K Ltd has chargeable profits of £15,000 for its accounting period ending on the same date and distributes £20,000 on that date of which £5,000 is made to Ms V who owns the remaining 25% of the company. There are no other associated companies involved. The corporation tax for the two companies is computed as follows.

J Ltd

J Ltd has no chargeable profits in the period and therefore, it has excess NCDs (in respect of the distribution of £12,000 to Mr T) which must be allocated as far as possible within the group or otherwise carried forward.

The profits available for allocated NCDs are K Ltd's profits of £15,000 less its NCDs of £5,000, i.e. £10,000. The maximum NCDs which can be allocated by J Ltd is 80% of that amount (the proportion that J Ltd's NCDs bear to its total distributions), i.e. £8,000. Accordingly, NCDs of £8,000 are allocated to K Ltd and £4,000 are carried forward.

K Ltd

		£
Non-corporate distributions		5,000
Matched to basic profits (note (b))	£15,000 × 25%	3,750
K Ltd excess NCDs carried forward		1,250
Profits chargeable to corporation tax	£15,000 @ 19%	2,850
Less: marginal relief (note (c))	(£25,000 − £15,000) × 19/400	475
Underlying corporation tax due		2,375
Underlying rate	(£2,375/£15,000) × 100	15.83%
K Ltd's own NCD		3,750
NCDs allocated by J Ltd		8,000
Total NCDs		11,750
Total distributions (note (d))		28,000
Corporation tax chargeable:		
On NCDs (11,750/28,000 × 15,000)	£6,295 @ 19%	1,196.05
Remaining profits at underlying rate	(£15,000 − £6,295) @ 15.83%	1,378.00
Total corporation tax due		£2,574.05

119.4 Non-Corporate Distribution Rate

Notes

(a)   If the distributing company is a member of a group at the end of the distribution period, any excess NCDs must be allocated, so far as possible, to other group companies. NCDs can only be allocated to other group companies to the extent they have 'available profits', i.e. their basic profits for an accounting period exceed their NCDs in that period. The maximum amount of NCDs which can be so allocated is that proportion of the recipient company's available profits that the distributing company's NCDs bear to its total distributions. In determining the amount of the recipient company's available profits at any time, account is only to be taken of the excess NCDs allocated to it before that time and still remaining with it.

(b)   The total distributions made by K Ltd of £20,000 exceed its basic profits of £15,000 so only 25% (NCDs £5,000 / total distributions £20,000) = 25%) of the profits, i.e. £3,750 (25% × £15,000) are matched with the NCDs. Since the excess NCDs of £1,250 cannot be allocated to another company, they are carried forward to the next accounting period.

(c)   There are two associated companies so the starting companies' upper limit for marginal relief is halved to £25,000.

(d)   Once NCDs are allocated to a recipient company, the recipient company is treated as having made that NCD in the period in which it is allocated in adddition to any NCDs it has made in its own right. The NCD rate is applied to that company as calculated in 119.3 above after the allocation has been made (HMRC Company Taxation Manual, CT3013).

(e)   See also note (a) at 119.1 above.

120   Payment of Tax

Cross-reference. See 110.1(B) and (C) and 113.2(A) and (B) for interest on overpaid and unpaid tax, and 123.1 and 123.2 for returns and filing dates.

120.1   **PAYMENTS BY LARGE COMPANIES** [*TMA 1970, ss 59D, 59E; FA 1998, s 30; SI 1998 No 3175; SI 1999 No 1929*]

(A) Large companies
BG Ltd, which has five associated companies, draws up accounts to 31 December each year. Its taxable profits and tax liabilities are as follows

Accounting period ended	Profits	Tax
	£	£
31.12.01	240,000	22,500
31.12.02	260,000	20,000
31.12.03	275,000	25,000
31.12.04	255,000	4,500
31.12.05	270,000	78,000
31.12.06	260,000	80,000
31.12.07	200,000	60,000

Assuming that the upper relevant maximum limit does not change, this will be as follows

£1,500,000 ÷ 6 = £250,000

Year ended 31.12.01
The company is not large as its profits do not exceed the upper maximum relevant limit.

Year ended 31.12.02
Although the company's profits exceed the upper maximum relevant limit, it will not have to make quarterly instalments payments because it was not large during the previous twelve months.

Year ended 31.12.03
The company is a large company in this period as it would have been a large company in the previous year but for the exclusion in *SI 1998 No 3175, reg 3*.

Year ended 31.12.04
Although the company's profits exceed the upper maximum relevant limit, its tax liability does not exceed £5,000 so it is not a large company.

Year ended 31.12.05
Although the company's profits exceed the upper maximum relevant limit, it will not have to make quarterly instalment payments because it was not large during the previous twelve months.

Year ended 31.12.06
The company is a large company in this period as it would have been a large company in the previous year but for the exclusion in *SI 1998 No 3175, reg 3*.

Year ended 31.12.07
The company is not large as its profits do not exceed the upper maximum relevant limit.

120.1 Payment of Tax

Notes

(*a*) A company is 'large' for the purpose of quarterly instalment payments, if its profits for an accounting period exceed the *ICTA 1988, s 13* 'upper relevant maximum amount' which is in force at the end of that period. This is currently £1,500,000 divided by one plus the number of associated companies. It is proportionately reduced where the accounting period is less than 12 months. 'Profits' mean profits chargeable to corporation tax plus franked investment income received otherwise than from other group members.

(*b*) A company is not large in an accounting period for which its total corporation tax liability (reduced by any deductions from payments in the period under the construction industry tax scheme) does not exceed £10,000, proportionately reduced if the accounting period is less than twelve months, or if its profits do not exceed £10,000,000 provided it was not a large company (disregarding this exclusion) in the previous 12-month period.

(B) Instalment payments – transitional period

HP Ltd draws up accounts to 30 September each year. Its taxable profits, and the tax due are as follows

Accounting period ended	Profits	Tax
	£	£
30.9.99	2,500,000	762,500
30.9.00	3,000,000	900,000
30.9.01	3,500,000	1,050,000
30.9.02	4,000,000	1,200,000

Tax is due and payable by the company as follows

Accounting period ending 30.9.99

		£
Instalments	due 14.4.99, 14.7.99, 14.10.99, 14.1.00 (£726,500 @ 60%/4 = £114,375 each)	457,500
Balance for 30.9.99	due 1.7.00	305,000
		£762,500

118

Accounting period ended 30.9.00

		£
Instalments	due 14.4.00, 14.7.00, 14.10.00, 14.1.01 (£900,000 @ 72%/4 = £162,000 each)	648,000
Balance for 30.9.00	due 1.7.01	252,000
		£900,000

Accounting period ended 30.9.01

		£
Instalments (@ 88%)	due 14.4.01	231,000
	due 14.7.01	231,000
	due 14.10.01	231,000
	due 14.1.02	231,000
Balance	due 1.7.02	126,000
		£1,050,000

Accounting period ended 30.9.02

		£
Instalments for 30.9.02	due 14.4.02	300,000
	due 14.7.02	300,000
	due 14.10.02	300,000
	due 14.1.03	300,000
		£1,200,000

Notes

(a) For accounting periods ending on or after 1 July 1999, 'large' companies (see note (c)) are required to pay corporation tax by instalments. Instalments are due at intervals of three months commencing six months and thirteen days from the start of the accounting period and culminating three months and fourteen days from its end. Therefore, for a twelve-month accounting period there will be four instalments.

(b) Instalment payments are calculated by reference to the total liability of the accounting period to which they relate. For accounting periods ending between 1 July 1999 and 30 June 2000, 60% of the liability is payable by instalments, for those ending between 1 July 2000 and 30 June 2001, 72% is so payable, and for those ending between 1 July 2001 and 30 June 2002, 88%. In each case the balance becomes due on the existing due date, i.e. nine months and one day from the end of the accounting period. For accounting periods ending on or after 1 July 2002, 100% of the total liability is payable by instalments. Each instalment is calculated by reference to the formula

$$3 \times \text{CTI}/n$$

where CTI is the total liability (or percentage thereof) and n is the number of whole calendar months in the accounting period plus the 'relevant decimal' (which adjusts for any odd days in the period).

(c) See notes (a) and (b) at (A) above for the definition of a 'large' company.

121 Profit Computations

121.1 COMPUTATIONS

Y Ltd's accounts for the 12 months to 31 December 2006 show the following.

	£		£
Wages and salaries	77,500	Gross trading profit	209,160
Rent, rates and insurance	5,000	Net rents	1,510
Motor expenses	8,000	Government securities	340
Car hire	6,000	Dividend from UK company	
Legal expenses	2,000	(received 30.9.05)	4,500
Directors' remuneration	22,875	Profit on sale of investment	5,500
Audit and accountancy	2,500		
Miscellaneous expenses	2,600		
Debenture finance charges	2,450		
Ordinary dividend paid	15,000		
Depreciation	6,125		
Premium on lease written off	14,000		
Net profit	56,960		
	£221,010		£221,010

Analysis of various items gave the following additional information

(i) Legal expenses:

	£
Re staff service agreements	250
Re debt collecting	600
Re new issue of debentures (see (viii) below)	1,150
	£2,000

(ii) Miscellaneous expenses:

	£
Staff outing	400
Subscriptions: Chamber of Commerce	250
Political party	100
Interest on overdue tax	250
Contribution to training and enterprise council	350
Charitable donation to trade benevolent fund	150
Other charitable donations	1,100
	£2,600

(iii) On 1 July 2006, Y Ltd was granted a lease on office accommodation for a period of seven years from that date for which it paid a premium of £14,000.

(iv) Car hire of £6,000 represents the hire, under a contract dated 1 July 2006, of a car with a retail price when new of £18,000 which is not a low-emissions car.

(v) All wages and salaries were paid during the period of account apart from directors' bonuses of £20,000, accrued in the accounts, voted at the AGM on 1 November 2007 and not previously paid or credited to directors' accounts with the company.

(vi) Profit on sale of investment is the unindexed gain arising from the sale of quoted securities on 28 February 2006. The chargeable gain after indexation is £2,070.

(vii)   Capital allowances for the year to 31 December 2006 are £10,000.

(viii)   Debenture finance charges relate to £50,000 nominal stock issued on 1 January 2006 for trade finance at £96 per £100, carrying interest at 4.5% payable annually in arrears, for redemption 31 December 2013. The charge to profit and loss comprises interest of £2,250 and redemption reserve costs of £200 on a straight line basis. As these are arrived at under an amortised cost basis, the charges are allowable for tax purposes. The issue costs included in legal expenses (see (i) above) are also allowable.

The £340 Government securities credit relates to £4,000 nominal stock acquired in May 2004 at £4,040 with two years to redemption. It represents gross interest £360 less £20 premium amortisation charge on a straight line basis. It is thus properly chargeable under Schedule D, Case III as a non-trade credit. The interest was received gross on 31 March and 30 September.

The corporation tax computation is as follows

	£	£
Net profit		56,960
Add		
Depreciation	6,125	
Directors' remuneration (note (*a*))	20,000	
Subscription to political party	100	
Charitable donations (notes (*c*) and (*d*))	1,100	
Car hire (note (*e*))	1,000	
Dividend paid	15,000	
Premium on lease written off	14,000	
Interest on overdue tax (note (*g*))	250	57,575
		114,535
Deduct		
Net rents	1,510	
Government securities	340	
Dividend received	4,500	
Profit on sale of investment	5,500	11,850
		102,685
Deduct		
Capital allowances	10,000	
Allowance for lease premium		

$$\frac{1}{7} \times \left(£14,000 - \left(\frac{7-1}{50} \times £14,000\right)\right) \times \frac{6}{12} \qquad 880$$

	£
	10,880
Schedule D, Case I trading profit	91,805
Schedule D, Case III (note (*g*))	90
Schedule A	1,510
Chargeable gains	2,070
	95,475
Deduct Charges paid — charitable donations	1,100
(note (*d*))	
Profits chargeable to corporation tax	£94,375

121.1 Profit Computations

Notes

(*a*)   Director's remuneration of £20,000 is disallowed as it remained unpaid nine months after the end of the period of account. It will, however, be allowable in the tax computation for the year to 31 December 2007, i.e. the period of account in which it is paid. [*FA 1989, s 43*]. See *ITEPA 2003, s 18* as applied by *FA 1989, s 43(6)* as to the time when remuneration is treated as paid.

(*b*)   The contribution to a training and enterprise council is allowable under *ICTA 1988, s 79A*.

(*c*)   The charitable donation to trade benevolent fund is allowable under *ICTA 1988, s 577(9)*.

(*d*)   The other charitable donations are allowable as charges on income under the Gift Aid provisions. [*ICTA 1988, ss 338(1)(2)(b), 339*].

(*e*)   The allowable proportion of the car hire expenditure is

$$\frac{£12,000 + £18,000}{£36,000} \times £6,000 = £5,000$$

[*ICTA 1988, ss 578A, 578B; CAA 2001, Sch 2 para 52*].

(*f*)   The proportion of the lease premium allowable is calculated under *ICTA 1988, ss 34(1), 87*.

(*g*)   Interest on the overdue tax is treated as a non-trading loan relationship debit. The Schedule D, Case III profit for the year ended 31 December 2005 is therefore (£340 − £250 =) £90.

121.2 **ALLOWANCE FOR CHARGES ON INCOME** [*ICTA 1988, ss 338, 393(9)*]
X Ltd, a UK resident company, made a Schedule D, Case I profit of £5,000 in the year to 31 October 2005 and had Schedule A income of £7,000.

It paid the following charges (shown gross)

	Situation (i) £	Situation (ii) £
Annual payments (other than interest)		
paid 31 January 2005	5,000	500
paid 31 July 2005	5,000	500
Donations to charity	4,000	13,000

The corporation tax position is

	£	£
Schedule D, Case I	5,000	5,000
Schedule A	7,000	7,000
	12,000	12,000
Deduct: management expenses	(5,000)	(500)
	7,000	11,500
Charges on income		
£9,000/£13,500, restricted to	7,000	11,500
Chargeable profits	Nil	Nil
Excess charges carried forward (note (*a*))	£2,000	£500
Unrelieved donations to charity		£1,500

Notes

(*a*) Excess charges on income can only be carried forward to the extent that they are incurred wholly and exclusively for the purposes of the trade.

(*b*) Annuities or other annual payments (not being in respect of loan relationships (e.g. interest) or royalties within the intangible assets regime) have been removed by *F(No 2)A 2005* from the classification of charges on income in relation to payments made on or after 16 March 2005. Such payments made on or after that date are deductible as management expenses where they meet the requirements for such expenses. This is subject to transitional provisions to prevent the same payment from being deducted twice. All that now remains as a charge on income, for payments on or after 16 March 2005, are qualifying donations to charities and certain gifts of shares and securities to charities and these are treated as non-trade charges. (Before the introduction of the intangible assets regime on 1 April 2002, any royalty or other sum in respect of the user of a patent was also treated as a charge on income.) [*F(No 2)A 2005, s 38*].

(*c*) See 118.1, 118.2 and 118.3(A) LOSSES for interaction between charges and various loss reliefs, and 110.6 GROUPS OF COMPANIES for interaction between charges and group relief.

122 Research and Development

122.1 SMALL OR MEDIUM-SIZED ENTERPRISE [*FA 2000, Sch 20 paras 13–20, 23; FA 2003, s 168, Sch 31*]

D Ltd is a small or medium-sized enterprise established on 1 January 2005. The company incurs qualifying research and development expenditure of £80,000 in the year ended 31 December 2005, in addition to other revenue expenditure of £50,000 (all of which would have been allowable expenditure had the company been trading). The company's total PAYE and NIC liabilities for payment periods ending in the accounting period are £15,000. On 1 January 2006 D Ltd commences a trade derived from the research and development expenditure, making a taxable profit (before adjustment for research and development relief or pre-trading expenditure) of £130,000 for the year ended 31 December 2006. Further qualifying research and development expenditure is incurred in that year of £41,000. The corporation tax position is as follows.

Y/e 31.12.05

D Ltd may elect, by 31 December 2007, to be treated as having incurred a trading loss in the period of an amount equal to 150% of the qualifying research and development expenditure, i.e. £120,000 (£80,000 × 150%). There are then four possible alternatives open to D Ltd to make use of the loss. It may:

(1) set the loss against other profits for the accounting period under *ICTA 1988, s 393A(1)(a)*;

(2) surrender the loss as group relief;

(3) claim a research and development tax credit equal to 16% of the loss (as reduced by any part of it relieved under (1) or (2)) or, if less, equal to the company's PAYE and NIC liabilities for payment periods ending in the accounting period; or

(4) carry the loss forward for set-off against future trading income under *ICTA 1988, s 393*.

D Ltd claims a tax credit as in (3) above in respect of the deemed loss for the year ended 31 December 2005. The maximum credit would be £120,000 × 16% = £19,200, but is restricted to £15,000, being the company's total PAYE and NIC liabilities for payment periods ending in the accounting period. Accordingly, part of the loss can still be carried forward (as in (4) above), amounting to £26,250 (£120,000 − (£15,000 × 100/16)).

Y/e 31.12.06

D Ltd claims for the qualifying research and development expenditure for the year to be treated as if it were 150% of the actual amount, i.e. £61,500. The company's taxable trading profits for the year are therefore as follows.

	£
Adjusted profit as above	130,000
Less Research and development relief	20,500
Other pre-trading expenditure	50,000
Schedule D, Case I profit	59,500
Less Loss brought forward	26,250
Trading profits chargeable to CT	£33,250

Note

(a) Relief for expenditure on research and development is available for expenditure of a revenue nature of at least £10,000 (reduced pro-rata for accounting periods of less than 12 months) incurred in accounting periods beginning on or after 27 September 2003 by a 'small or medium-sized' company on qualifying 'research and development'. The minimum expenditure limit was £25,000 for accounting periods beginning before that date for expenditure incurred on or after 1 April 2000. A 'small or medium-sized' enterprise is one that has less than 250 employees and either or both annual turnover not exceeding 50 million euros (or, for accounting periods ending before 1 January 2005, 40 million euros) and annual balance sheet total not exceeding 43 million euros (or, for accounting periods ending before 1 January 2005, 27 million euros). A company is generally excluded if any company in which it holds, or which holds in it, more than 25% of the capital or voting rights, is not a small or medium-sized enterprise.

(b)   *FA 2002, Sch 12* introduced a research and development relief for large companies (i.e. companies which are not small or medium-sized enterprises as defined in (*a*) above). Where such companies incur qualifying research and development expenditure of not less than £10,000 per annum after 9 April 2003 (£25,000 before that date and after 31 March 2002), they may claim an additional trading deduction of an amount equal to 25% of the expenditure. [*FA 2002, Sch 12 para 11*]. Tax credits, as claimed by D Ltd for the year ended 31 December 2003, are not available to such companies. *FA 2002* also introduced a new relief for expenditure on research into certain vaccines, which is available to any company, and may be claimed in addition to any research and development relief available in respect of the expenditure concerned. [*FA 2002, Sch 13*].

123 Returns

123.1 **RETURN PERIODS** [*FA 1998, Sch 18 paras 3–7*]

(A)

Aquarius Ltd has always prepared its accounts to 31 October. In 2006, it changes its accounting date, preparing accounts for the nine months to 31 July 2006. On 31 January 2006, HMRC issues a notice specifying a return period of 1 November 2004 to 31 October 2005. On 31 January 2007, they issue a notice specifying a return period of 1 November 2005 to 31 October 2006.

In respect of the first-mentioned notice, Aquarius Ltd is required to make a return for the period 1.11.04 to 31.10.05 accompanied by accounts and tax computations for that period.

In respect of the second of the above-mentioned notices, the company is required to make a return for the period 1.11.05 to 31.7.06 accompanied by accounts and tax computations for that period. [*FA 1998, Sch 18 para 5(1)(2)*].

(B)

Pisces Ltd has always prepared its accounts to 31 December. In 2006, it changes its accounting date, preparing accounts for the nine months to 30 September 2006. On 15 December 2006, HMRC issue a notice specifying a return period of 1 October 2005 to 30 September 2006.

Pisces Ltd is required to make returns both for the period 1.1.05 to 31.12.05 and for the period 1.1.06 to 30.9.06, each return being accompanied by accounts and tax computations for the period covered by it. [*FA 1998, Sch 18 para 5(1)(2)*].

Note

(*a*)   The company may need to obtain an additional return form from HMRC.

(C)

Aries Ltd has always prepared accounts to 31 October. After 2005, it changes its accounting date, preparing accounts for the fifteen months to 31 January 2007. On 21 August 2006, HMRC issue a notice specifying a return period of 1 November 2004 to 31 October 2005. On 31 January 2007, they issue a notice specifying a return period of 1 November 2005 to 31 October 2006.

In respect of the first-mentioned notice, Aries Ltd is required to make a return for the period 1.11.04 to 31.10.05 accompanied by accounts and tax computations for that period.

In respect of the second of the above-mentioned notices, the company is required to make a return for the accounting period 1.11.05 to 31.10.06, accompanied by accounts and tax computations for the period of account 1.11.05 to 31.1.07. [*FA 1998, Sch 18 para 5(1)(3)*].

(D)

Taurus Ltd has always prepared accounts to 31 October. After 2005, it changes its accounting date, preparing accounts for the fifteen months to 31 January 2007. On 31 January 2006, HMRC issue a notice specifying a return period of 1 November 2004 to 31 October 2005. On 1 April 2006, HMRC issue a notice specifying a return period of 1 November 2005 to 31 January 2006.

In respect of the first-mentioned notice, the position is as in (C) above.

In respect of the second of the above-mentioned notices, Taurus Ltd is not required to make a return, but should notify the Revenue of the correct accounting dates and periods. [*FA 1998, Sch 18 para 5(3)(5)*].

(E)

Gemini Ltd was incorporated on 1 July 2003 but remains dormant until 1 April 2005 when it begins to trade. The first trading accounts are prepared for the year to 31 March 2006 and the company retains that accounting date. On 1 May 2007, HMRC issue notices specifying return periods of 1 July 2003 to 30 June 2004, 1 July 2004 to 30 June 2005, 1 July 2005 to 30 June 2006 and 1 July 2006 to 31 March 2007.

In respect of the notice for the period 1.7.03 to 30.6.04, Gemini Ltd is required to make a return for that period.

In respect of the notice for the period 1.7.04 to 30.6.05, the company is required to make a return for the period 1.7.04 to 31.3.05. [*TMA 1970, s11(2)(b); F(No 2)A 1987, s 82(3)*].

In respect of the notice for the period 1.7.05 to 30.6.06, the company is required to make a return for the period 1.4.05 to 31.3.06 accompanied by accounts and tax computations for that period.

In respect of the notice for the period 1.7.06 to 31.3.07, the company is required to make a return for the period 1.4.06 to 31.3.07 accompanied by accounts and tax computations for that period. [*FA 1998, Sch 18 para 5(1)(2)*].

123.2 Returns

123.2 **FILING DATES** [*FA 1998, Sch 18 para 14*]
The final dates for the filing with HMRC of the returns in 123.1 above, and for the payment of corporation tax (assuming none of the companies concerned falls within the definition of a 'large company' to which the instalment payment provisions apply—see 120.1(A) PAYMENT OF TAX), are as follows

Return period	Filing date		Payment date (note (*f*))
123.1(A) above			
1.11.04 – 31.10.05	31.10.06	(note (*a*))	1.8.06
1.11.05 – 31.7.06	31.7.07		1.5.07
123.1(B) above			
1.1.05 – 31.12.05	15.3.07	(note (*b*))	1.10.06
1.1.06 – 30.9.06	30.9.07		1.7.07
123.1(C) above			
1.11.04 – 31.10.05	21.11.06	(note (*b*))	1.8.06
1.11.05 – 31.10.06	31.1.08	(note (*c*))	1.8.07
123.1(D) above			
1.11.04 – 31.10.05	31.10.06		1.8.06
123.1(E) above			
1.7.03 – 30.6.04	1.8.07		—
1.7.04 – 31.3.05	1.8.07		—
1.4.05 – 31.3.06	1.8.07		1.1.07
1.4.06 – 31.3.07	31.3.08		1.1.08

Notes

(*a*) The normal filing date is the first anniversary of the last day of the return period.

(*b*) If later than the date in (*a*) above (or, where relevant, (*c*) below), the filing date is three months after the date on which the notice is issued by the Inspector.

(*c*) Where a company's period of account extends beyond the end of the return period, the filing date is extended to the first anniversary of the last day of that period of account. This is subject to a limit of 30 months from the beginning of the period of account, although this would come into play only in the exceptional case where accounts are prepared for a period exceeding 18 months.

(*d*) The time allowed for filing returns is effectively extended to the time allowed under the *Companies Act 1985* if this would give a later filing date than under (*a*)–(*c*) above. [*FA 1998, Sch 18 para 19*]. This will not be so in the majority of cases.

(*e*) HMRC may grant an extension, on an application by the company, if they are satisfied that the company has a 'reasonable excuse' for not being able to meet the filing date under (*a*)–(*c*) above. [*TMA 1970, s 118(2); F(No 2)A 1987, s 94*].

(*f*) Nothing in (*a*)–(*e*) above affects a company's liability to pay corporation tax within nine months and one day following the end of an accounting period. [*ICTA 1988, s 10(1)(a)*]. See 120.1(B) PAYMENT OF TAX for the instalment payment provisions applicable to large companies.

124   Small Companies—Reduced Rates

124.1 **REDUCED RATE IF PROFITS £300,000 OR LESS — MARGINAL RELIEF** [*ICTA 1988, s 13; FA 1994, s 86; FA 2004, s 26*]

(A)

In its accounting period 1 April 2006 to 31 March 2007, X Ltd, a trading company, has chargeable profits of £300,000 including chargeable gains of £40,000, and also has franked investment income of £75,000 (representing net distributions received of £67,500). X Ltd has no associated companies.

Corporation tax payable is calculated as follows

	£
Corporation tax at full rate of 30% on £300,000	90,000
$\frac{11}{400} \times £(1,500,000 - 375,000) \times \dfrac{300,000}{375,000}$	24,750
Corporation tax payable	£65,250

Note

(*a*)   Marginal relief applies as profits, including franked investment income, fall between the lower and upper limits of £300,000 and £1,500,000 respectively.

(B)

In its accounting period 1 April 2006 to 31 March 2007, Y Ltd, a trading company, has chargeable profits of £375,000 including chargeable gains of £40,000, but has no franked investment income. Y Ltd has no associated companies.

Corporation tax payable is calculated as follows

	£
Corporation tax at full rate of 30% on £375,000	112,500
$\frac{11}{400} \times £(1,500,000 - 375,000)$	30,938
Corporation tax payable	£81,562

Note

(*a*)   An alternative method of calculation, where there is no franked investment income, is to apply small companies rate up to the small companies rate limit and marginal rate (32.75% for FY 2006) to the balance of profits. Thus

	£
£300,000 at 19%	57,000
75,000 at 32.75%	24,562
£375,000	£81,562

124.1 Small Companies—Reduced Rates

(C) Changes in the marginal relief fraction [*ICTA 1988, ss 8(3), 13(3)(6); FA 1994, s 86*]

In its accounting period 1 January 2002 to 31 December 2002, Z Ltd had chargeable profits of £540,000 and franked investment income of £60,000. Z Ltd had no associated companies.

Corporation tax payable is calculated as follows

Part of the accounting period falling in financial year 2001

			£	£
Profits	$\frac{3}{12} \times £600,000$	= £150,000		
Basic profits $\frac{3}{12} \times £540,000$		= £135,000		
Lower relevant maximum		= £75,000 (note (*b*))		
Corporation tax at full rate £135,000 at 30%			40,500	
Less marginal relief				
$\frac{1}{40} \times £(375,000 - 150,000) \times \dfrac{135,000}{150,000}$			5,063	35,437

Part of the accounting period falling in financial year 2002

			£	£
Profits	$\frac{9}{12} \times £600,000$	= £450,000		
Basic profits $\frac{9}{12} \times £540,000$		= £405,000		
Lower relevant maximum		= £225,000 (note (*b*))		
Corporation tax at full rate £405,000 at 30%			121,500	
Less marginal relief				
$\frac{11}{400} \times £(1,125,000 - 450,000) \times \dfrac{405,000}{450,000}$			16,706	104,794
Corporation tax payable				£140,231

Notes

(*a*) Where the marginal relief fraction changes from one financial year to the next, an accounting period which overlaps the end of the first such year is treated as if the part before and the part after were separate accounting periods.

(*b*) The relevant maximum and minimum amounts are proportionately reduced for an actual or notional accounting period of less than twelve months.

Upper relevant maximum amount
Financial year 2001 $\frac{3}{12} \times £1,500,000 =$ £375,000
Financial year 2002 $\frac{9}{12} \times £1,500,000 =$ £1,125,000

Lower relevant maximum amount
Financial year 2001 $\frac{3}{12} \times$ £300,000 = £75,000
Financial year 2002 $\frac{9}{12} \times$ £300,000 = £225,000

124.2 **STARTING RATE—MARGINAL RELIEF** [*ICTA 1988, s 13AA; FA 1999, ss 28, 29; FA 2002, s 32; FA 2006, s 26*]

(A)

In its accounting period 1 April 2005 to 31 March 2006, X Ltd, a trading company, has chargeable profits of £10,000, including chargeable gains of £400, and also has franked investment income of £2,500 (representing net distributions received of £2,250). X Ltd has no associated companies.

Corporation tax payable is calculated as follows

	£
Corporation tax at small companies rate of 19% on £10,000	1,900
$\frac{19}{400} \times £(50,000 - 12,500) \times \dfrac{10,000}{12,500}$	1,425
Corporation tax payable	£475

Note

(*a*)   Marginal relief applies as profits, including franked investment income fall between the first and second limits of £10,000 and £50,000 respectively.

(*b*)   The starting rate was introduced from the financial year 2000 and was abolished from the financial year 2006. The rate is 0% for financial years 2002 to 2005 and 10% for financial years 2000 and 2001.

(B)

In its accounting period 1 April 2005 to 31 March 2006, Y Ltd, a trading company, has chargeable profits of £12,500, including chargeable gains of £400, but has no franked investment income. Y Ltd has no associated companies.

Corporation tax payable is calculated as follows

	£
Corporation tax at small companies rate of 19% on £12,500	2,375
$\frac{19}{400} \times £(50,000 - 12,500)$	1,781
Corporation tax payable	£594

Note

(*a*)   An alternative method of calculation, where there is no franked investment income, is to apply the starting rate up to the starting rate limit and the marginal rate (23.75% for FY 2005) to the balance of profits. Thus

	£
£10,000 at 0%	—
2,500 at 23.75%	594
£12,500	£594

(*b*)   See note (*b*) to (A) above.

124.3 Small Companies—Reduced Rates

124.3 **A COMPANY WITH AN ASSOCIATED COMPANY OR COMPANIES** [*ICTA 1988, s 13(3)–(7); FA 1994, s 86*]

(A)

C Ltd has a 51% subsidiary, D Ltd. Both companies are resident in the UK. C Ltd had previously prepared accounts to 31 March but changes its accounting date and prepares accounts for the nine-month period to 31 December 2006. Its chargeable profits for that period amount to £480,000. It also receives franked investment income of £84,000 including £24,000 representing dividends from D Ltd. At no time in the accounting period to 31 December 2006 does C Ltd have any active associated companies other than D Ltd.

Corporation tax payable by C Ltd for the period to 31 December 2006 is calculated as follows

	£
Corporation tax at full rate of 30% on £480,000	144,000
$\frac{11}{400} \times £(562,500 - 540,000) \times \dfrac{480,000}{540,000}$	550
Corporation tax payable	£143,450

Notes

(a) The relevant maximum and minimum amounts are proportionately reduced for accounting periods of less than twelve months and further reduced where the company has associated companies (other than dormant ones) at any time during the accounting period.

Upper relevant maximum amount
$\frac{9}{12} \times \frac{1}{2} \times £1,500,000 = £562,500$

Lower relevant maximum amount
$\frac{9}{12} \times \frac{1}{2} \times £300,000 = £112,500$

(b) Profits for these purposes do not include distributions from within the group. [*ICTA 1988, s 13(7); FA 1998, Sch 3 para 7*]. Thus, the £24,000 franked investment income received from D Ltd is omitted from the calculations in this example.

(B) Changes in relevant maximum amounts

A Ltd has chargeable profits of £200,000 for the 12-month accounting period ended 30 September 1994 and has no franked investment income. It had no associated company until 1 March 1994 when all of its share capital was acquired by a company, B Ltd, with three wholly-owned subsidiaries, of which one was dormant throughout the 12-month period and another was resident overseas. B Ltd acquired a further active subsidiary on 1 May 1994.

Corporation tax payable by A Ltd is calculated as follows

Part of the accounting period falling in financial year 1993

		£	£
Profits $\frac{6}{12}$ × £200,000	= £100,000		
Lower relevant maximum	= £31,250 (note (*b*))		
Upper relevant maximum	= £156,250 (note (*b*))		
Corporation tax at full rate £100,000 at 33%		33,000	
Less marginal relief			
$\frac{1}{50}$ × £(156,250 − 100,000)		1,125	31,875

Part of the accounting period falling in financial year 1994

		£	£
Profits $\frac{6}{12}$ × £200,000	= £100,000		
Lower relevant maximum	= £30,000 (note (*b*))		
Upper relevant maximum	= £150,000 (note (*b*))		
Corporation tax at full rate £100,000 at 33%		33,000	
Less marginal relief			
$\frac{1}{50}$ × £(150,000 − 100,000)		1,000	32,000
Corporation tax payable			£63,875

Notes

(*a*)   Where the relevant maximum amounts change from one financial year to the next, an accounting period which overlaps the end of the first such year is treated as if the part before and the part after were separate accounting periods.

(*b*)   The relevant maximum and minimum amounts are proportionately reduced for an actual or notional accounting period of less than twelve months and also where the company has associated companies (other than dormant ones) at any time during the accounting period.

Upper relevant maximum amount
Financial year 1993 $\frac{6}{12} \times \frac{1}{4} \times$ £1,250,000 = £156,250
Financial year 1994 $\frac{6}{12} \times \frac{1}{5} \times$ £1,500,000 = £150,000

Lower relevant maximum amount
Financial year 1993 $\frac{6}{12} \times \frac{1}{4} \times$ £250,000 =   £31,250
Financial year 1994 $\frac{6}{12} \times \frac{1}{5} \times$ £300,000 =   £30,000

(*c*)   Small companies relief and marginal relief are not given automatically, but must be claimed. The claim must include a statement of the number of associated companies, or a statement that there were none, in the relevant accounting period. (Revenue Statement of Practice SP 1/91). The claim may be made by completing the relevant boxes of the corporation tax return.

125   Transfer Pricing

125.1 **ADJUSTMENTS FOR TRANSFER PRICING** [*ICTA 1988, Sch 28AA; FA 2004, ss 30–37, Sch 5*].

(A) Transfer pricing adjustment

A Ltd provides management and administrative services to a number of its wholly-owned subsidiaries. All companies in the group have accounting periods ending on 31 March and do not qualify as small or medium-sized enterprises for transfer pricing purposes. For the accounting period ending 31 March 2007, A Ltd makes a charge for its management and administrative services to B Ltd of £450,000. Following an enquiry into A Ltd's return for that period, it is agreed that the arm's length value of the services to A Ltd was £600,000. An adjustment is accordingly made of £150,000 to increase A Ltd's taxable profits by that amount.

B Ltd can claim to apply a corresponding adjustment (see note (*d*) below) to reduce its taxable profits for the same period by £150,000 (increasing its deductible expenses to £600,000). B Ltd may also make a balancing payment to A Ltd of up to £150,000 without it being treated as a distribution or charge on income or otherwise taken into account for tax purposes.

Notes

(*a*)   The transfer pricing rules apply broadly where transactions between connected parties take place at other than arm's length prices conferring an advantage to the of the parties in terms of a reduction in the liability to UK tax. A transfer pricing adjustment may then be made to restore the tax position to what it would have been had the transaction been at arm's length. For accounting periods beginning on or after 1 April 2004 (with transitional rules for accounting periods straddling that date), the transfer pricing regime is extended to apply to both UK and cross-border transactions. Dormant companies and small and medium-sized enterprises will, in most circumstances, be exempt from applying the transfer pricing and thin capitalisation rules. Where an adjustment is required by the provisions to increase the profits of one party, the corresponding adjustments provisions are extended so that the connected UK party can make a compensating reduction in their taxable profits, and new provisions allow for a 'balancing payment' to be made tax-free up to the amount of the compensating adjustment.

(*b*)   Where an accounting period of a company straddles 1 April 2004, it is treated, for the purposes of calculating the company's profits and losses, as two separate accounting periods, the first ending on 31 March 2004 and the second, to which the new rules apply, beginning on 1 April 2004.

(*c*)   A 'dormant' company is one which is dormant (under the *Companies Act 1985, s 249AA(4)–(7)*) throughout the accounting period ending on 31 March 2004 (or if there is no such accounting period, the three-month period ending on that date); and has continued to be dormant at all times since the end of that period apart from any transfer pricing adjustments. Very broadly, a small enterprise is defined as a business with less than 50 employees and either turnover or assets of less than €10 million and a small or medium-sized enterprise as a business with less than 250 employees and either turnover of less than €50 million or assets of less than €43 million. A medium-sized enterprise can still be subject to a transfer pricing notice.

(*d*)   Where a transfer pricing adjustment has been made by the advantaged party (either in the return or following a determination) the disadvantaged party may claim a corresponding adjustment in applying the arm's length rather than the actual provision. Claims must be made within two years of the making of the return or the giving of the notice taking account of the determination, and a claim based on a return which is subsequently the subject of such a notice may be amended within two years of the giving of the notice. (These time limits may be extended in certain cases where the Board fails to give proper notice to disadvantaged persons under *FA 1998, s 111(3)*.)

(e)   Where a transfer pricing adjustment is made, the disadvantaged company may make a corresponding balancing payment to the advantaged company. Provided the balancing payment does not exceed the amount of the 'available compensating adjustment', it is not taken into account when computing profits or losses for tax purposes or regarded as a distribution or charge on income. The *'available compensating adjustment'* is the difference between the profits and losses of the disadvantaged company computed on the basis of the actual provision and computed for the purposes of making a compensating adjustment (see note (d) above).

(B) Transfer pricing and thin capitalisation

On 1 July 2006, B Ltd is granted a loan of £5,000,000 at 6% interest p.a. from an unassociated bank. The loan is guaranteed by B Ltd's parent company, G plc. Both companies draw up accounts for the year ended 30 June and neither company qualifies as a small or medium-sized enterprise for transfer pricing purposes. Following an enquiry into B Ltd's return for the accounting period ending 30 June 2006, HMRC successfully maintain that, in the absence of the guarantee from G plc, the bank would not have advanced more than £1,000,000 to B Ltd. Accordingly, an adjustment is made to increase B Ltd's profits for the period by £240,000 in disallowing the interest on £4,000,000 of the loan.

G plc could make a claim (or B Ltd could claim on its behalf) for a corresponding adjustment before or after the transfer pricing adjustment is made in B Ltd's return, or following the determination so that it is treated as having paid the interest subject to the disallowance. Accordingly, provided the interest in G plc's case would not be subject to a transfer pricing adjustment, G plc could claim a deduction for £240,000 in respect of the interest paid by B Ltd. G plc can make a balancing payment of up to £240,000 to B Ltd without it being treated as a distribution or charge on income or otherwise taken into account for tax purposes.

Notes

(a)   For accounting periods beginning on or after 1 April 2004, the thin capitalisation rules in *ICTA 1988, s 209(2)(da), (8A)–(8F)* (whereby excessive payments of interest by companies which are thinly capitalised are treated as distributions) are repealed and are instead subsumed within the extended transfer pricing regime (see (A) above). New rules apply for guarantors of third party loans, and exemption from deduction at source under *ICTA 1988, s 349* can be claimed.

(b)   A compensating adjustment may be claimed by the disadvantaged party or by the advantaged person his behalf (a paragraph 6C claim) before or after the arm's length provision has been applied in the case of the advantaged party (in his return or following a determination). Where a transfer pricing adjustment to disallow interest follows from the provision of a guarantee, the guarantor can claim a compensating adjustment as if it was the borrower and had paid the interest subject to the disallowance, and adjust its accounts accordingly. A claim can also be made by the lender on behalf of the guarantor. Claims must be made or amended before the expiry of the time limits in note (d) to (A) above.

(c)   Where a transfer pricing adjustment applies to disallow interest and the lendor claims a compensating adjustment under either *TA 1988, Sch 28AA para 6 or 6C*, the interest disallowed as a deduction for the borrower is correspondingly not treated as Schedule D Case III income for the lending company. (The condition for deduction at source in *TA 1988, s 349(2)* is therefore not met so that where a paragraph 6C claim is made (see above) the borrowing company can pay interest to a not-resident lender without deduction of tax at source.).

(d)   Where a transfer pricing adjustment applies in the case of the advantaged company, the guarantor company may make a corresponding balancing payment to the borrower. Provided such a balancing payment does not in aggregate exceed the amount of the compensating adjustment, it is not taken into account for corporation tax purposes when computing profits or losses of the guarantor or the borrower, or regarded as a distribution or charge on income. The compensating adjustment in this case is the total reduction in interest or other amounts payable under the loan subject to the guarantee (and thus treated as paid by the guarantor).

(e)   See also the notes to (A) above.

Table of Statutes

Table of Statutes

Table of Statutes

Table of Statutory Instruments

Index

Index

This index is referenced to chapter and paragraph number within the five main sections of the book. The entries in bold capitals are chapter headings in the text.

Index